A DIALOGUE *of* COMFORT AGAINST TRIBLUATION

ST. THOMAS MORE

CLUNY

Providence, Rhode Island

A DIALOGUE *of* COMFORT
AGAINST TRIBULATION

CONTENTS

BOOK III : The Third Conversation: On Persecution

"All fortune is good fortune; for it either rewards, disciplines, amends, or punishes, and so is either useful or just."

Boethius, *The Consolation of Philosophy*

BOOK I

The First Conversation: Foundational Matters

INTRODUCTION

Vincent pays a visit to his kinsman Anthony.

VINCENT: Who would have thought, dear uncle, even just a few years ago, that here in Hungary someone who was visiting an old or a sick friend would come as I am now doing to find comfort for *themselves*? Priests and friars call upon the sick to give comfort to *others*, to help them remember death, while we more worldly friends, out of a desire not to make the sick uneasy, have always tried to lift up their hearts and give them hope for continuing life.

But now things have so changed and there is so much danger surrounding us that I am coming to think that the best comfort a man can have is to know that he will soon be dead. We who are likely to continue living in such wretchedness need the comfort of good counsel against all this tribulation from someone like you, good uncle. You have lived a long and virtuous life, and are well versed in the ways of God. You have had a wide experience of the things we now fear, for you were twice a prisoner in Turkey; and you are now soon to depart from this life.

It may be a great consolation to you that you will soon go to God. But you will leave us, your kinfolk, like a pack of unhappy orphans. Your help, encouragement, and counsel have long been a source of great strength to us, as if you were not only an uncle or even a more distant relative, but a true father to each one of us.

ANTHONY: My good cousin, I cannot deny that not only here in Hungary, but throughout Christendom, the kind of unchristian comfort you just mentioned is indeed the custom. It does a sick man more harm than good to keep his mind away from meditating on death, judgment, heaven, and hell, matters he should be thinking about during the whole of his life, even when he is in good health. And that kind of "comfort" seems to me close to madness when it comes to a man of my advanced age. For if it is true that a young man *may* die soon, it is certain that an old man *will*. But as Tully has said, there is no man who is so old that he does not hope for one more year of life, and who does not try to comfort himself with such folly. When others come and speak to him in the same foolish way, they add more sticks to the fire and burn away the pleasant dew that should refresh him—I mean the grace of God leading him to desire to be with God in heaven.

As for your sorrow at my departure, I only wish that I had done half as much for you and for others as was my duty. But if you were to think yourself without comfort if God should decide to take me, it would be like throwing away a strong staff and leaning on a rotten reed. God is and must be your true comfort, not I. He is a sure comfort, and never leaves his servants as orphans even when he departs from them. He sent them a comforter, the Holy Spirit, and he promised that he would dwell with them to the end of the world. If you are one of his flock and you believe his promises, how can you be without consolation, no matter what the trial may be, when Christ, his Holy Spirit, and the Father himself—if you put your trust in them—are never an inch of space or a moment of time away from you?

VINCENT: Uncle, these very words of yours about God's comfort are making me feel how much we will miss your comfort when you are gone. For while I agree wholeheartedly with what you have said, I would not have remembered it if you had not reminded me. Since our trials are certain to grow, we will be needing not only one or two encouraging words like these, but many of them, if we are to keep the walls of our hearts strong and stable against the surges of this tempestuous sea.

ANTHONY: Cousin, put your trust in God and he will provide suitable teachers for whatever you need, or else he will teach you by inward ways.

VINCENT: Granted, uncle. But if we were to turn away from a teacher when he is available and look to be taught only inwardly by God, we would displease him by our presumption. I know that when you are gone we will not have another like you. So once again I make the request: in the short time that remains to us let us learn from you how best to weather the storms of suffering that my family and friends are already encountering, and that will only grow worse with the coming of the cruel Turk upon us. Then, by remembering your words I may be able to steer the ship of our family and keep it afloat in the midst of the coming spiritual storm.

For you are well aware, uncle, of the sufferings that many in our family have already encountered, of such magnitude that I find myself without words of comfort for them. And now, as the news of the Great Turk's plans to invade this territory has broken upon us, we can hardly speak or think of anything but his power and our danger. We see in our mind's eye his mighty strength, his malice and hatred, and his incomparable cruelty. Our hearts are filled with fearful visions of his robbing, spoiling, burning and laying waste everything he comes across, of his killing or making captives of the populace, dividing married couples and families, keeping some in slavery and killing some in his presence. Then he will send his own people to preach false beliefs, and many of us will either lose the faith and be lost, or will be forced by coercion to forsake Christ and embrace the false sect of Mohammed. What we fear most is already happening: many of our own people are falling prey to him, or have made alliance with him, joining him ahead of time as a way of keeping him from ravaging the land. We will be in great danger if that happens, for there is no born Turk so cruel to Christian folk as false Christians who fall away from the faith. We will either be carried away as slaves to Turkey, or die a yet more cruel death at the hands of our own countrymen. Our fear is so great in the face of these dangers that many of us recall the prophecy of our Savior concerning Jerusalem, and wish that the mountains would overwhelm us or the valleys open up and swallow us before the peril comes upon us.

And so, good uncle, I have come to ask you to give us as much of your wise counsel as you can, to be weapons against these horrible fears, so that I can write it down and keep it with me when God will have called you away.

ANTHONY: All you say makes a heavy hearing, cousin. And I suspect that just as we are now filled with fear over what we did not fear at all even a few years ago, many others will soon come to fear what they think cannot harm them because they dwell farther away.

When I was young, Greece did not fear the Turk; but soon that empire was his. The Sultan of Syria thought himself more than a match for the Turk, but that land has been taken too. He has since captured Belgrade, the outpost of this realm, and killed our noble young king. Then came the fall of the strong fortress of Rhodes, which he counted as a victory against the whole of Christendom, since all Christendom was unable to defend that island against him. If the Christian princes had been united, the Turk would never have taken any of those places. But partly due to our own divisions, and partly because no one seems to care much for what happens to others, the realm of the Turk has grown greatly in just a few years, and Christendom has sadly declined. And all this has happened because our wickedness is so displeasing to God.

But now as I consider our many reasons to fear, I myself begin to think that we need encouraging counsels against so many troubles. It so happens that just before you came I was thinking about the coming invasion of the Turk, and my mind flew to my own departure from this life. For though I trust in God and hope to be saved by his mercy, no one without a special revelation can be certain that he is safe. So I began to meditate on the pains of hell, and to compare those with the invasion of the Turk. At first the terror of his coming seemed to me almost nothing compared to the fearful dread of hell, with its fiendish tormentors and its furious endless fires. I considered that if the Turk and his whole army were to come to my bedroom door and kill me in my bed, when I compared his terrors to the joyful hope of heaven and the fearful pains of hell, I would hardly give him a thought. Yet now, as I hear your sad words, and think about what is likely soon to come upon us, I find myself all the more willing to help you preserve in your heart a store of consolation as a remedy against the desperate dread that may come upon you in your sufferings. I will be glad to call to mind with you, as much as my feeble wit is able, whatever I have read, heard, or thought about that may serve our purpose.

I.

The insufficiency of the consolations given
by philosophers.

FIRST, good cousin, you should know that the wise men of this
world, the old moral philosophers, labored long over this matter.
They recorded many natural reasons why we should set little store
by the goods of the world, whether we possess them or lose them.
I am speaking of things such as riches, favor, friends, fame, worldly
honor, and bodily goods like beauty, strength, agility, liveliness, and
health. Grief for the loss of these goods is what we commonly call
tribulation or suffering. It is true that when our bodies feel the loss
of physical goods, there is no train of thought that can make the pain
go away. But philosophers have worked hard to free the mind from
grief over such losses, and have gathered many wise sayings to urge
men to have contempt for the loss of worldly goods, and to despise
the pains of sickness, and even death itself.

Yet in all that I have read, I could never be convinced that their
natural reasons provided sufficient consolation against sorrow. For
they never reach the special point that is not only our main consolation, but the comfort without which all the rest means nothing.
I mean the confidence that by patiently suffering here we will gain
God's favor and receive a reward from him in heaven. Because the
men of old lacked this special knowledge of our true *end*, they could

not point to the *means* by which we could gain it; namely, the grace and help of God encouraging us toward heaven. As a result, all their words fall short of the mark.

Nonetheless, though these philosophers are unable entirely to cure our disease, and should not be taken as our physicians, they still have some good medicines in their shops, and we can use them as apothecaries to help fill out the prescriptions given by God, who is the true physician. So we will neither go along fully with their reasoning, nor utterly refuse them, but we will use them insofar as they correspond with the regimen of the excellent physician who alone can cure us of the deadly disease of damnation.

Let us then ask that divine physician, our blessed savior Christ, to cure our deadly wounds with the medicine made from the blood of his own blessed body. And let us further pray that as he has cured our mortal disease by his incomparable medicine, it may please him to put into our mind medicines that will strengthen us against the sorrows of suffering, so that our enemy the devil, with his poisoned darts of complaining, resentment, and impatience, may never have the power to turn our short sickness of suffering here into the endless death of hell.

II.

*Faith is the one foundation upon which
to build our consolation.*

SINCE our main consolation must come from God, we will first lay the only basis upon which our true comfort can be founded: namely, the ground of faith. Without it, nothing will help. Just as it would be useless to use natural reason with someone who had no mind, so it would be of no use to speak of spiritual consolations with someone who has no faith. Without faith, he cannot believe the Scriptures in which God has spoken words of comfort. The stronger his faith, the greater the consolation he can find in God's word.

No one can command faith; it is the gift of God. As St. James says, "Every good endowment and every perfect gift is from above, coming down from the Father of lights" (James 1:17). Let us then first pray that God give us a good measure of faith, taking as our example that man in the Gospel who said, "I believe Lord; help my unbelief!" (Mark 9:24). And in order to keep our faith from weakening and losing its vigor, let us tend the garden of our souls, and pull out the weeds that would get in faith's way. Then, as the small mustard seed of faith grows, it will spread out its branches and bring forth flowers of virtue, such that the birds of the air—the very angels of heaven—will dwell within our souls. Then we will be better able to withstand even a mountain of violent suffering and cast it out of our hearts; whereas when faith is weak, even a little hillock of suffering overwhelms us. So here is our first conclusion: before we can hope for any spiritual consolation we need to have faith; and since faith comes only from God, we need to call upon God ceaselessly for this precious gift.

VINCENT: It seems right to me, as you say, that faith needs to be the foundation of the rest, and that without it all spiritual comfort would be given in vain. I will willingly ask God for a full measure of it. And I ask you, uncle, to proceed further on your course.

ANTHONY: That I will gladly do, cousin.

III.

The first consolation: the desire to be comforted by God.

ANTHONY: Let us then speak of the first cause for consolation: the desire and longing to be consoled by God. A sick person who has no desire to get well is in a desperate state. The same is true of a suffering person who has no desire to find comfort in God. There are four types of people in this matter of suffering and desiring consolation: two who will not seek comfort at all, and two who seek comfort, some wrongly and some rightly.

Of those who do not seek any consolation, the first sort are people who are so drowned in suffering that they fall into a deadly dullness, regarding nothing, thinking almost nothing, and lying prostrate in a kind of lethargy. This comfortless kind of suffering is the worst expression of the deadly sin of sloth.

The second sort also do not seek consolation, and receive none. In their suffering these people become so angry, bitter, and impatient that it is impossible to speak with them. They sometimes become so furious that they fall into a frenzy. This comfortless response to suffering is the deadly sin of anger.

The third type of person does indeed seek comfort, but looks to the pleasures of the world for it. As St. Bernard once said, the one who turns to worldly vanities to escape suffering is like a drowning man who grabs whatever he can find and holds tight to it, even if it is only a stick of wood; and he and his stick go down together.

The fourth type are those we want to emulate: they long to be comforted by God himself. This is a source of great consolation to them, for two reasons. First, they are looking for consolation in just the place where it can be found. For God is both able and willing to give comfort. "Ask, and you shall receive" is the promise he made to us (Matt. 7). The one who has faith does not doubt that God will keep his promise.

There is yet a second source of consolation in the desire to be comforted by God. The person of faith knows that all good desires come from God, and all evil desires from the world, the devil, or ourselves. He sees that God has graced him with the good desire to have God for his comfort, and this is greatly encouraging to him, as a sign that God himself is at work in him for his salvation. He is then content to wait upon whatever consolation God might send, knowing that he has not been cast off from God's favor. So the very desire to gain comfort from God is itself a source of consolation.

IV.

Suffering as a means of drawing the mind toward longing for God's consolation.

VINCENT: May our Lord send us this longing for God's comfort in our suffering, uncle. I see clearly by your words that those who do not desire to be comforted by God in time of suffering are either slothful, angry, or running for comfort elsewhere, and are in deep trouble.

ANTHONY: Yes, cousin, that is true. But remember that one reason God sends suffering is precisely to drive them from that state. Though pain was ordained by God for the punishment of sins, yet when it comes upon us in this world, suffering is usually a means of repentance.

St. Paul himself fought against Christ until he was thrown to the ground and struck blind. God was acting as his physician through that suffering, and God soon healed him in both body and soul and made him his own apostle. Sometimes men who are very stubborn at the onset of suffering are brought home by it at last. The proud Pharaoh endured the first two or three plagues; but when God laid a sterner lash on him, he cried for help, confessed himself a sinner, and acknowledged the power and goodness of God. He then sent for Aaron and Moses and begged them to pray for him to withdraw the plague. Yet as soon as the suffering was withdrawn, he turned wicked again. The tribulation was profitable for him, and its withdrawal caused him harm. So it is that suffering often brings a person to seek consolation from God.

But it does not always work in this manner. Unless there is at least some consolation beforehand, suffering does not bring it forth. So we should consider by what means this initial consolation may come. If a person is running from God's consolations and has landed in sloth, anger, or intemperance, his friends who visit and counsel him should do what they can to help him realize his fault, and encourage him to ask God for the desire to be comforted by him, rather than spending their time (as they commonly do) in turning him to the illusions of this world. If they encourage him this way, I do not doubt that God in his goodness will give what they ask.

V.

*It is not enough to desire God's comfort only through
the removal of our suffering.*

VINCENT: I see your point, uncle. It can do no good to give spiritual counsel to a person who does not hope for help from God. But given the desire for God's consolation, what if the person desires to be comforted by asking God to take his suffering away? Is this a sufficient hope for someone in the midst of tribulation?

ANTHONY: I am afraid not, cousin. It is true that we may sometimes ask God to take our suffering away. But it does not apply in every case; and even when it does, relief from suffering cannot be properly asked for except under a certain condition, whether expressed or implied. As you know, tribulation comes in many forms. Some trials come from loss of our possessions, some from sickness or bodily pain, and some from the loss of friends. Some suffering may come not so much from the actual loss of these things as from the fear of losing them. And the worst kind of suffering is the fear of losing our immortal life by committing deadly sin.

It is obvious that we may pray to God to ask him to take from us much of this kind of suffering. Many of the prayers of the Church, even the Pater Noster itself, express this desire. Yet it is not true in every case. For example, if a person prays in every sickness that his health be restored, he will never be contented to see his life end and to depart to be with God; and yet that is a very necessary attitude. Again, it is a trial for a good person to face the inner battle, the relics of original sin in us, as his rebellious flesh rises against the rule and governance of his reason. Yet even St. Paul was not given the grace to have this kind of tribulation completely taken from him, since it is part of God's plan that we learn to fight against it with his strength, and to gain merit through mastering it.

We may boldly pray for the salvation of our souls. We may also confidently pray for grace, along with faith, hope, and charity, and for every other virtue that will help us toward heaven. But we should never pray for an end to our particular trials without expressing or implying this condition: that if God thinks it better for us to remain in a state of suffering, we will gladly leave the matter to his will and to his fatherly care. If such is the case, we should then pray to be given the consolation to take our suffering gladly, or at least the strength to bear it patiently. When we insist that the only consolation that will satisfy us is that we be freed from our suffering, we put ourselves in the false position of claiming to know what we need better than God himself. If we insist that we know what is best, we may foolishly choose what is worst. In the face of such presumption, God may be merciful and pay no attention to our request, or he may in indignation give us what we ask for, and we will find later that it has led to our harm.

How many people attain physical health who would be in a better state for the health of their soul if they remained sick? How many people get out of prison and then get into all kinds of trouble that prison would have kept them away from? How many of those who fear losing their worldly goods soon lose their very lives? We are so blind in our mortality, so unaware of what will befall us, and so unsure of what the state of our minds may be tomorrow, that God could hardly do a man more harm than to grant him his own foolish desires.

How can creatures like us know what will most help us? The blessed apostle Paul prayed to God three times that his suffering might be removed, and God answered him by saying that the help of divine grace in the midst of his trial was far better for him than removing it would have been. He warns us not to be too confident in thinking that we know what will be best for us. He says that "we do not know how to pray as we ought, but the Spirit himself intercedes for us with sighs too deep for words" (Rom. 8:26). Let us then never ask God to remove tribulation simply for the sake of our own ease of life; but instead let us pray for his aid and comfort through whatever ways he himself thinks best. We can be sure that this kind of thinking comes from God, and that he who has begun a good work in us will not cast us off. As St. Paul also said, "If God is with us, who can be against us?" (Rom. 8:31).

VI.

It is not enough to desire God's comfort only through the removal of our suffering.

VINCENT: I can see what kind of consolation we may pray for in the midst of suffering, uncle. But tell me: are there other spiritual consolations that can come from tribulation?

ANTHONY: I believe that there are great consolations in suffering, cousin. Every trial that comes upon us is either medicine for our souls, or may become such medicine if we will allow it, and may be even better than medicine for us if we willingly endure it.

VINCENT: That would indeed be a comfort! But it is hardly an obvious truth.

ANTHONY: Then let me explain. Every trial that comes upon us falls under one of the following three categories. It is either (1) suffering that we have brought upon ourselves, such as sickness from overeating or drinking too much or a prison sentence given us for some crime; or (2) it is sent from God as punishment for past sins or to preserve us from committing serious sins in the future; or (3) it is not due to our sins at all, but is meant to test our patience and to gain us merit in God's eyes. In all these cases our tribulation can be medicine for our souls; and in the last case, it is even better than medicine.

VII.

*Concerning comfort to be gained from tribulation
caused by our own known faults.*

VINCENT: This seems a good explanation, uncle. Can you go into further detail?

ANTHONY: Yes; let us take each of these instances of suffering and explain them more fully. As to those tribulations that come upon us from our own misdeeds, as when sickness follows gluttonous feasting or a man is punished for his own open fault: it may seem that they leave a man far from consolation. But he has good reason to be comforted in the midst of them, if only he determines to make a medicine of them. For whatever suffering might come from his sin, a far greater punishment is waiting in another world. Yet if a man humbly and patiently receives suffering in this world with faith and hope in Christ's passion, he has a medicine that is sure to cure him, and to remove the pains of the disease that would otherwise come upon him later. For God is good and does not punish the same thing twice.

Even if this punishment has come upon him by force rather than by free choice, and even though he would happily have avoided it if he could, still if he repents of his sin and recognizes his fault, God in his goodness counts the suffering as if it were a willing act of purgation and penitence. By this grace, God allows a man to make a virtue of necessity and a medicine of his malady, and the man comes to a good end.

Consider the story of Achan who committed sacrilege among the Israelites in the desert. When his sin was discovered by lot, Achan could see that he was found out and taken against his will. But when Joshua exhorted him to give glory to God and confess his fault, Achan humbly did so. I am sure that he found strength and comfort in the midst of his pain, and died a good man. Yet had he never been in peril and never been given the opportunity to express remorse, he might have died a wretched death and ended up with the devil eternally. Consider also the converted thief who hung at Christ's right hand. By the humble acknowledgement of his fault, by asking God's forgiveness and yet being content to suffer for his sin, he turned his just punishment and his well-deserved suffering into a potent medicine to cure him of all pains in the coming world, and by so doing he gained eternal salvation. That is why I insist that this kind of suffering, though it is in itself the least encouraging, can still become an excellent and wholesome medicine for those who make it so, and a reason for great spiritual consolation.

VIII.

*Concerning comfort to be gained from tribulation that
seems not to come from our known faults.*

VINCENT: You have opened my mind to understand this first kind
of suffering, uncle. Can we go on to the second?

ANTHONY: The second kind of suffering is the tribulation that
comes upon us for reasons that we do not know. But the truth is
that we seldom lack faults against God that deserve severe punishment. Even if we do not know what particular sin has brought on
the suffering, we are wise to think that we have deserved it. This way
of responding to tribulation is similar to the first, and it can bring
us the same kind of medicine. But for those who have been living
with a sober conscience and a clean life, there is yet more comfort
in this kind of suffering. For God sometimes sends trials to preserve
a person from sins into which he would otherwise fall. For such as
these there is a kind of double medicine from which they can gain
great consolation.

We call a medicine good when it restores us to health after we
have been sick. Yet an even better medicine preserves our health
while we still possess it and keeps us from falling into painful sickness. So it is with this better kind of spiritual medicine. For example, it may happen that God sees wealth coming quickly to a good

man, and knowing perfectly the man's weakness, God knows what he can handle and what he cannot, and he foresees a fall into pride and vanity. So in his goodness God sends the man ahead of time some kind of trial that helps him see the vanity of this false flattering world. God sets a cross upon the ship of his heart and teaches him to carry a low sail, so that the boisterous blast of pride does not blow him under the water. Or here is a lovely young wife, and well-meaning too; yet God sees that if her health and her fine fat feeding last only a little longer she will fall into a lecherous love, and instead of being true to her long-acquainted knight, will crawl into bed with a newly-acquainted knave. But God loves her too tenderly to allow her to fall into such a beastly sin, and so he sends a strong fervent fever that makes her bones rattle and her wanton flesh waste away. It turns her fair skin to the color of a buzzard's claw, and gives her the sort of "loveliness" that her lover will hardly look at. It so affects her lustful desires that if her lover were to lay in her lap, the only intimacy she could manage would be to throw up in his face.

So you see, cousin, that suffering can be a double medicine: both a cure for past sins and a preservative from sins that are to come. It is therefore a source of double consolation, depending on the state of the conscience of each person.

IX.

Concerning comfort to be gained from tribulation that comes, not from our sins, but for our merit.

VINCENT: Very good, uncle. Now only the third kind of suffering remains: the kind that is not due to sins we have committed or as a prevention from sins to come, but is sent to exercise our patience and increase our merit. But I cannot see how there would be more consolation in this case, since every man has sin enough on his conscience to think that his suffering is sent as punishment.

ANTHONY: There is truth in what you say, cousin, and it will be enough for the majority of men to take consolation in their suffering as a punishment for past or possible future sins. I would not advise just anyone to go further than this. But there are some, though few, whose lives and consciences are such that—despite being sinners— they can take some hope of consolation from the thought that God is sending them trials not so much for their punishment as for the exercise of their patience. St. Paul was one such, as was Job. And apart from these examples of conscientious living, there are some sources of trial that I would without a doubt ascribe to this last kind of tribulation.

VINCENT: What kinds of trials fall into that category, uncle?

ANTHONY: Whenever a man suffers to maintain justice or to defend the cause of God. If I saw a man who had led a virtuous life fall into the hands of the Turk, and who testified to the truth despite torture and torment, and if I was in a position to give him spiritual counsel, I would not hesitate to tell him that he should throw sin, hell, purgatory and all into the devil's face, and that—even though his merit would be lost should he abandon the faith—if he only persevere, in his good confession, all his pain would be turned into glory.

A man who suffers in the cause of justice, who chooses to defend the right even to his own hurt, can gain great comfort in the clearness of his conscience. Especially one who has been falsely accused of a crime and has had false witnesses rise against him, and who is punished and shamed before the world for it. He may have a hundred times more consolation than pain in his heart. Such are the consolations of a man who abides by the truth and is persecuted for justice during a time when white is called black, and right is called wrong.

I will go even further. Imagine that there was a Christian man living among infidels who had committed a deadly sin worthy of death, such as murder or adultery, and who was offered pardon on condition that he should abandon Christ. If he were to suffer death rather than give over his faith, I would tell him that even though he was dying for his sin, he was dying for Christ. By forsaking his own life to honor his faith, God would forgive the pain of all his sins and reward him with heaven's life—all through the merits of Christ's passion, without which no suffering of our own has merit. And though this man had once been a devilish sinner, he would be taken for a martyr among Christians.

VINCENT: So in the cause of defending what is right, if a man sues me and wrongly tries to take my property, can I then find comfort in upholding my rights, and expect gratitude from God for it?

ANTHONY: Careful, cousin; there you are somewhat wide of the mark. In that case you are defending your right in a way that leads to your own temporal good. Remember that St. Paul advises, "Do not defend yourselves" (Rom. 12:19), and our Lord says, "If a man takes your coat, give him your cloak as well" (Luke 6:29). Defending our own right does not bring a special reward. You are doing well enough to get permission from God to defend yourself; don't be asking for thanks!

On the other hand, if you follow St. Paul's injunction to look not only to your own interests but to those of others, and you defend a poor widow or a fatherless child and suffer at the hands of a wealthy extortioner, or if you invite the malice of a powerful man because you will not judge wrongly in his favor, then the blessing of Christ falls to you, as he said: "Blessed are those who are persecuted for justice, for theirs is the kingdom of heaven" (Matt. 5:10). There is great consolation in such a case. When a man knows his conscience to be clear, the spiritual joy that fills his heart may far surpass whatever heavy grief he has experienced by the loss of some temporal good.

VINCENT: I can see, good uncle, that this third kind of consolation is greater than the first two kinds you have spoken of.

ANTHONY: Very right, cousin; and yet even the lowest kind of trial, that which is sent to us for sins we have committed or to keep us from sins we may yet commit, brings more reasons for spiritual comfort than I have yet mentioned. Suffering in hell is punishment pure and simple since the possibility of purgation is past; and in purgatory suffering is for purging alone since the possibility of gaining merit is past. Yet in this world, if we take suffering for our sins in faith, not only will it purge us and cleanse our guilt; it will increase our heavenly reward. And so will all those works of penance that a man willingly performs, either given by his spiritual father in confession, or arising from his own devotion. Though our penances are not able to satisfy the least of our sins on their own, God is so good that he will reward us for them beyond what we can now imagine through the merits of Christ's bitter passion. And this also is a cause of great consolation.

X.

An objection raised concerning what has been said about merit gained in tribulation.

VINCENT: I find these thoughts comforting indeed, uncle. Yet as you know, there are many who now deny that our suffering on earth can diminish the pains of purgatory in any way; and others who go so far as to say there is no purgatory at all. If they are right, the source of our consolation has disappeared. The same people also say that we can merit nothing, and that God gives everything to us by faith alone; and that it would be sin and sacrilege to look for a reward in heaven either for patiently suffering for God's sake, or for doing any good deed at all. So according to their account all our comfort vanishes.

ANTHONY: Yes, cousin, it is true that lately these opinions and many others have been spread abroad. It is sad to see divisions arise and grow among us, such that our common enemies are encouraged to think that they will be able to overwhelm us in the midst of our fighting. Yet I have some hope that we may yet find a way to unity of mind. And even now in Germany, where so many divisions exist, they are coming together in defense of Christendom to battle our common enemy the Turk. So I will leave behind any bitter contention and entrust everything to the hands of God; I will only speak to the issues you have raised.

As for the existence of purgatory: though these people think there is no purgatory, they still cannot deny that the whole body of Christendom for hundreds of years has thought the contrary, among them venerable interpreters of Scripture from the time of the Apostles down to our own, many of whom these same people take to be holy and good. So I hope they will courteously excuse me if I dare not believe them against the testimony of all these others. And I heartily pray that when they themselves depart from this wretched world they do indeed find that there is no purgatory in store for them—provided God keep them from hell!

As for the merit a man gains by his good works: those who deny it do not agree with one another, and there is hardly one of them who has not changed his views since his writing began. In any case, there is more agreement here than it might sometimes seem. For we willingly grant to them the following points: that good works are worth nothing at all without faith; that a good work is considered good not from its own nature but through the goodness of God, who has been pleased to put a high value on so lowly a thing through the worth of Christ's passion; that any good work we accomplish is only the work of God within us; and further that no man can be proud of his works, since they are always imperfect and he is only an unprofitable servant who is barely doing his duty and can do no good of himself. And they grant us a few things in return: that men are bound to do good works if they have the power, and that those who act with the truest faith will be most highly rewarded. But they then further add that the reward a man receives will be given to him for his faith alone and not for his works, since his faith is that which forces him to do good works. I will not contend with them over this matter, and only say that if the question hangs on that subtle point, I will trust in the great goodness of God. And I will believe that since the Scripture says in so many places that we will be rewarded in heaven for our good works, God will not allow us—who after all are dimwitted men who can only understand things as he himself has put them in Scripture and as holy saints and all the Christian people have believed for a thousand years and more—to be damned for not perceiving such a fine distinction.

Beyond that there are many learned people with very sharp minds who cannot see why these others insist that our reward is to come only from faith and not from charity, which is what good works mean. These say instead that faith itself is worth nothing unless it is accompanied by her sister charity. The Scripture itself says, "Faith, hope, and charity abide; but the greatest of these is charity" (1 Cor. 13:13). It would seem that charity is as worthy of reward as faith. Yet I will not fight for this point, since my purpose here is to speak of our sources of heavenly comfort; and whether one receives a high reward for good works or for well-working faith, comfort is still to be had, and that is the purpose of our conversation.

VINCENT: Thank you, uncle. This way of putting things answers my question well. So I would ask you to continue your good counsel.

XI.

*Complete absence of suffering is not a good sign
of God's favor.*

ANTHONY: There are so many sources of consolation in our suffering, cousin, that it would be hard to enumerate them all. But I think we will be able to see better what these are by looking at the harm the lack of tribulation brings, and the kind of desolation it leaves to those who do not have it.

All the saints, the whole of Scripture, and our own experience all agree that we are not in this wretched world to make it our home. As Scripture says, "Here we have no lasting city, but we seek the city which is to come" (Heb. 14:13). It says further that we should seek that city; for I fear that those who do not care for it enough to seek it will never attain it. "Run," we are told, "so that you may win it" (1 Cor. 9:24). If it can only be won by running, what are we to say of those who will not lift a foot to get there?

Because this world is not our eternal dwelling, but only our little-while wandering, God desires that we deal with it as if we were weary of it. He desires that while we are in this valley of labor, toil, tears, and misery, we do not look for rest and ease, for games, pleasure, wealth, or happiness. Those who do so act like that foolish fellow who is on his way toward his own home where he will inherit great wealth, but who stops along the road and takes a job caring for horses at an inn for the sake of a pint of beer, and so dies in a stable, never getting home at all.

Our Savior has said: "Woe to you who laugh now, for you shall mourn and weep" (Luke 6:25). And in another place the Scripture says, "There is a time to weep, and a time to laugh" (Eccl. 3:4). As you see, the weeping comes first, because that is the time of this wretched world, and the laughing comes after in heaven. There is a time for sowing and a time for reaping. In this world we sow, that we may reap in the next. And in the short sowing time of this world, we water our seed with the showers of our tears. We shall then have a merry laughing harvest forever in heaven. "They went out weeping, sowing their seed," says the prophet. But what followed? "They came back more than laughing, in great joy and exultation, with heaps of grain in their hands" (Ps. 126:6). So it is: those who make their way to heaven sowing their seed with weeping, will come back to their bodies on the day of judgment with abundant laughter. As if to prove that this life is not a time of laughing, but rather of weeping, we find that our Savior himself wept two or three times, while he never laughed even once. I will not swear that he never did; but at least he left us no example of it, as he did with weeping.

We have matter enough to weep about for our own sins and for those of others too. For surely we should weep and bewail the sins of others, and not happily denounce them or envy them. Poor souls; what is there to envy in those who are wealthy and without trial in this world? Job has said of such people: "They spend their days in prosperity, and in peace they go down to Sheol" (Job 21:13). St. Paul says that God chastises those he loves, "and he scourges every son he receives" (Heb. 12:6). He also says, "By many trials we must gain the Kingdom of God" (Acts 14:22). No surprise in this, for our

Savior Christ said to the two disciples on the road to Emmaus, "Did you not know that the Christ must suffer, and by that means enter into his kingdom?" (Luke 24:26). And do we, his servants, look to be treated with more privilege in the master's house than the Master himself? Shall we gain his kingdom with ease when he himself only gained it with pain? "If any man would come after me, let him deny himself and take up his cross and follow me" (Matt. 16:24). If heaven is reserved for Christ's disciples, and if Christ's disciples are those who take up their cross of suffering, how will those who have not suffered make their way to heaven? If what Scripture says is true, that God chastises all whom he loves and scourges every child he receives, and that heaven is the place for those he loves and receives, how can anyone gain heaven who has never been chastised by him, and who has never received so much as a lash? If it is true that we can only come into the kingdom through tribulation, how will those who do not suffer ever make it there? So we can see by the very voice of Scripture how true are the words of the saints, who have all said with one voice that we cannot have continual good fortune both in this world and in the next. Those who enjoy a long course of uninterrupted prosperity in this world without any suffering have great cause to fear that they are not in God's favor, but instead are deep in his indignation and displeasure. For it would seem that he never sends them the suffering that comes to those he loves. On the other hand, those who are in the midst of tribulation have good reason for inward comfort and spiritual consolation amid their grief.

XII.

An objection concerning certain counsels of the learned.

VINCENT: I find your words convincing, uncle. Yet you speak very strongly about people who enjoy continual prosperity. There are many such people, including those who have the rule of the world in their hands. And when these men in authority go to the wise and learned to ask whether they can both be merry all their lives on earth and still gain heaven, those learned men are eager to tell them "Yes!" I have heard such talk myself.

ANTHONY: I don't suppose, cousin, that any truly wise man, especially if he is also a good man, will speak that way. Those who do so are only flattering the wealthy, whether for love of money or for fear of loss. I suspect that some of them think along these lines: "This powerful man makes much of me, and pays me to fast and pray for him. But if I told him that he also needed to fast and pray for himself, he would not be happy. And if I went further and said that I trusted that my own diligent intercession on his behalf would be the means by which God would send him the grace to repent, and to fast and pray and do penance for the saving of his soul, he would be very angry with me. He does not want any grace from God that would make him stop his merry-making and bring him to mourn for his sins." Many of the learned think this way, and so they perilously beguile influential men for fear of losing their money and their worldly position.

And there are others who tell such tales due to a different fear. Seeing the man so bent on his own pleasure, and despairing of any amendment in his behavior no matter what they might say, and seeing also that the man seems to do no great harm, but instead courteously does some good, they ask God to send him grace to repent sometime in the future. They leave him lying lame in his fleshly desires at the pool of Bethesda spoken of in the Gospel where the crippled waited to see if the waters would stir. They hope that at some future time the angel will stir the waters of his soul, and they will then be ready to help him plunge into the pool of penance. But meanwhile, lest the man grow worse rather than better, and turn from a sweet and courteous disposition to a rough and sour one and so be a great trouble to everyone, they speak fair and comforting words to him, and let him take his own chances.

They act like a mother whose young son has overslept and is late for school. He is anxious and crying because he will be punished by the schoolmaster. She tells him that he is not to worry: "Go along to school, son. I have sent a message to the master myself. Take your bread and butter with you—you shall certainly not get a beating!" If she can just send him away from her door happy, she hardly cares whether he gets beaten when he reaches school. I fear that many friars and chaplains do the same sort of thing in giving comfort to great men whom they do not want to displease.

XIII.

Further objections raised concerning prosperity
and tribulation.

VINCENT: But uncle, though some certainly do this, it does not resolve the deeper question. For the whole Church in its services regularly has us pray that God would send health and prosperity, especially for rulers and bishops, but more generally for everyone, and even for ourselves. I can't imagine a good man asking God to send sorrow upon another person, and as far as I know there are no such prayers in the breviaries of the priests. Yet if what you say is true, if continual prosperity is dangerous to the soul and tribulation is so good for it, then it would seem that everyone would be bound in charity not only to pray that God send suffering upon his neighbor, but even to participate in bringing the suffering about. They would not pray for the sick to get better; instead they would say: "I am glad, good friend, that you are so sick—and I pray that God will keep you in that state for a long time!" According to that way of thinking, no one should give medicine to another or take any himself, since by diminishing his suffering he would take away what would profit his soul.

And besides, good uncle, we read in Scripture of men who were both wealthy and good. Solomon was the richest king of his time, and yet he was beloved by God. Job also was no beggar; and though

God took his wealth from him, he did so not because he did not want Job to be wealthy, but so that Job could practice patience and shame the devil. As proof that prosperity can be a divine gift, God restored to Job double of all that he had lost, and gave him a long life during which he could enjoy his prosperity. And when poor Lazarus died in our Lord's parable, the best place to which he could come was to a rich man's bosom in the figure of Abraham!

And finally, good uncle, we see before our eyes that there are many people who are wealthy and yet very good, while many of the impoverished are as evil as they are poor. So it seems to me difficult to say that suffering is always given by God to those he loves as a sign of their salvation, and that prosperity is a sign of displeasure and a token of eternal damnation.

XIV.

The objections answered.

ANTHONY: I did not say, cousin, or at least I did not mean to say, that it is a consistent rule that worldly prosperity is always displeasing to God or that tribulation is wholesome for every person at all times. I know well enough that our Lord sometimes brings suffering and sometimes good fortune on both good and evil men, for "he makes the sun shine on both the good and the bad, and his rain to fall on the just and the unjust" (Matt. 5:45). He may give evil people good fortune in this world to call them through kindness. Yet when wealth will not bring them, he sometimes lands them in sorrow and suffering. Some who cannot even creep forward to God when they are prosperous run fast toward him when they suffer trials. God sends wealth to some good people who give him thanks for his gifts; and to some good people he sends sorrow, and they thank him for that too. If God gave good things only to evil people, it would seem that God was not the just ruler of the world. And if God gave good things only to good people, many would serve him only to gain good fortune. For some people, prosperity leads to folly, as the Psalm says, "Man cannot abide in his pomp; he is like the beasts that perish" (Ps. 49:12). For others, suffering leads to sin, and so the Psalm says, "For the scepter of wickedness shall not rest upon the land allotted to the righteous, lest the righteous put forth their hands to do wrong"

(Ps. 125:3). So either state, prosperity or suffering, may lead to either virtue or vice.

But that is not precisely the point we have been discussing. The question is not whether good fortune is always a dangerous sign; but rather, whether continual prosperity in this world without tribulation is a sign of God's indignation. That is the target we must shoot at, and we must consider whether your arrows are near or far from the mark.

VINCENT: Yes, uncle, I understand. Let me then pick up some of my arrows and put them back in my quiver, since I see that I did not have the target clearly in my mind.

ANTHONY: Let me first pick up for you some of the arrows you shot at the target and that landed too short. First, you argued that perpetual wealth is not an evil token, since we pray for prosperity in the common prayers of the Church. Second, you suggested that if prosperity were really so dangerous, we should ask God to send suffering on others. Third, you brought forward the examples of Solomon, Job, and Abraham. And fourth, you noted that we see by daily experience that some wealthy people are good, and some needy folk are very wicked. This last one I have just spoken to, and I think we can pick that arrow up. Let us see what we can do with the other three.

Our first need, if we are to hit the target, is to know what we mean by tribulation or suffering. I suppose you will agree that suffering refers to something that troubles or grieves a person either physically or mentally; it is like the prick of a thorn or a briar thrust into his flesh or into his mind. And I think it is true to say that the thorn that pricks the mind is far more troubling than the grief that pains the body.

If this description of tribulation is accurate, then see what follows: there are more kinds of suffering than you have perhaps considered before. And this also follows: that since any kind of suffering is an interruption of prosperity, our wealth can be taken from us in more ways than it might at first seem. So, cousin, I would insist on this: since tribulation touches not only the body but also the mind, many good men suffer in ways that others cannot see, and their prosperity is hindered without it being known to anyone else. Just think: are not the temptations of the world, the flesh, and the devil that clamor to move the mind of a good man to commit sin a great inward suffering of the heart? Wretches who don't care at all about their consciences and who follow their desires like so many irrational beasts find this kind of temptation no trouble at all; it is even a source of pleasure. But the person who fears God finds the suffering of temptation so painful that he would happily give half of everything he owns or more, if only he could be rid of the temptation or be sure that he would be victorious over it. If someone who cares nothing for God wants to understand the nature of this kind of suffering, let him consider the kind of suffering he himself endures when his desire is thwarted—say, when he is after a good woman who will not allow herself to be caught. Then let him say whether his desire will not so torment his mind that every other pleasure leaves him cold if he cannot gain that one. Just as piercing is the pain of a good man in his battle against temptation and his fear of falling into sin.

If such suffering from temptation is indeed a great tribulation, and therefore a kind of interruption of prosperity, then no one would pray simply that another be kept in continual good fortune without any change. If there were no other condition added or implied to that prayer, it would mean that we would be childishly praying that the person would either never experience temptation, or never resist it so as never to suffer! Who could make such a request of God?

Then too, cousin, the Church advises every person to fast, watch, and pray both for subduing fleshly desires and to ask forgiveness for sins, as the people of Nineveh did in Jonah's day, and as David did at the bidding of the prophet Nathan. Are these practices not to be called suffering just because the man happens to do them to himself? If another forced him to do them, we would surely call it suffering, and he does indeed suffer, though he does it with a very good will. So whenever we find the prayers of the Church asking God for good fortune, we may be sure that these prayers never mean to keep a good man—or a bad one for that matter—from every kind of tribulation. And so I answer your first objection.

Now before I tackle your second objection, I will move to your third concerning the wealthy men of Scripture, since the solution to the objections you have raised will depend on it.

As for Solomon, you say that he was wealthy all his days, and I know that he was much beloved by God early in his reign. But it is not clear that his favor with God lasted as long as his prosperity, so I will not simply grant it. Surely it was his continual wealth that led him into wanton folly, first by multiplying his wives to a horrible number contrary to God's law, and then by taking among his wives some who were infidels, again disobeying a commandment of God. And by means of his infidel wife he eventually fell into idolatry himself. We have no record of his repentance of this idolatry, as we have of his father David after he had fallen into sin. Whether through some secret sorrow for his sins—which is to say by some kind of suffering—he found at last the place of rest that his father did, I cannot say, and I am content to trust and pray that he did. But we cannot be sure of it, and therefore your example of Solomon cannot help your case. You might as well say that God favors idolatry as that he favors prosperity; for Solomon was both prosperous and idolatrous.

As for Job, since our question has to do with perpetual prosperity, Job's wealth cannot be a good example, since it was interrupted with terrible adversity. The fact that God gave him double what he had lost does not touch my argument, which does not deny that God is the giver of prosperity, or that he gives it to good men who have also experienced suffering.

But I suppose your strongest example is Abraham, cousin, because in him we see not only riches and prosperity through the whole of his life, but after his death too. The poor man Lazarus had comfort and rest after a life of pain and hunger in that wealthy man's bosom. But here we must understand that Abraham did not live in continual prosperity; instead he was regularly troubled with various trials.

Was it nothing to him, do you think, to leave his own country and be sent into a strange land, of which, though it was promised to his descendants, he was never given even a square foot for himself? Was it no trouble that he had to part with his cousin Lot because their servants could not get along? Though he was able to recapture Lot from the three kings who had abducted him, was this no trouble to him? Did the destruction of the five cities bring no heaviness of heart to him? Anyone reading that story, and seeing how hard he tried to save them, could hardly think so. I would guess that he found sorrow in being forced to let Abimelech the king have his wife

Sarah. And what a continual grief was it to him, day after day, that he had no child of his own! His complaint to God is registered in the book of Genesis. No doubt the birth of Ishmael was a great comfort to him; but was it then no suffering to have to cast the child out from his home along with his mother? And what of the sacrifice of his son Isaac? Who can even conceive what heaviness of spirit he experienced as he prepared to kill his own son at God's command? Since you have been speaking of Lazarus, I would guess that Lazarus' own death was not as painful as this. Just as Lazarus bore his suffering patiently, so did Abraham, and with even greater merit, since it came from willing obedience. One should rather say that Abraham suffered even more than Lazarus. And this is your example!

But cousin, let us examine a little more carefully the story of the rich Abraham and the poor Lazarus. Think of that other figure, that rich man calling and crying from his fiery bed for Lazarus to cool the tip of his burning tongue with a drop of water. What then does Abraham say to that rich wretch? "Son, remember that you in your lifetime received your good things, and Lazarus in like manner evil things; but now he is comforted here, and you are in anguish" (Luke 16:25). Jesus described the wealth of the man vividly: he fared royally every day; his clothes were soft and costly, and his wealth was continual. Now he and Lazarus have exchanged places, the one from wealth to suffering, the other from suffering to wealth. Yet we are not told of any great virtue belonging to Lazarus, nor of any great vice clinging to the rich man: only that he took his continual ease with no grief, because of which he grew negligent about the sufferings of others. We do not even know if he ever saw Lazarus, or knew that he had died of hunger at his door. Neither Christ nor Abraham lays that to the rich man's charge. So this story is an excellent example of the danger of continual worldly prosperity, and also of the comfort that can come from tribulation. If the examples of Solomon and Job have not exactly helped your case, this example of Abraham and Lazarus has hindered it a good bit.

XV.

Further answers to the objections.

VINCENT: Well, uncle, you have certainly shaken my examples, and I see that my arrows were even wider off the mark than I thought. I'll willingly pick them back up. But it seems to me that my second arrow may still be on target. For if it is true that suffering brings such good with it, why would we ever wish or pray or do anything to have our trials taken away from us or from our friends?

ANTHONY: I do indeed think that suffering brings great good with it, and like you I might wonder why any of us should pray or labor to be delivered from it, except that God who teaches us to take our suffering with patience also teaches us to pray and to do what we can to relieve our suffering and that of our neighbor. Since God teaches both, we need not break our heads over the matter.

So for instance, if we are facing a great famine, God wills that we bear it patiently; yet he wants us to eat our food when we can get it. If a plague of pestilence is going round, he wants us to take it patiently; but he does not forbid us from taking medicine or asking the help of physicians. The Scripture teaches both of these attitudes in many places. Fasting is better than eating and brings more graces, but God still wants us to eat. Praying is better than drinking and much more pleasing to God, and yet God bids us drink. Keeping vigil is more acceptable to God than sleeping, and yet it is not displeasing to God that we sleep.

God has given us bodies that we might care for them and serve him in them, until the time comes when he takes us from this life. We cannot easily tell how much bodily suffering we can handle, and when it might harm our bodies or even our souls. That is why the Apostle Paul, after he had instructed the Corinthians to excommunicate the adulterous offender who had taken his own father's wife (1 Cor. 5), then told them to receive him back once he had been punished for his sin lest "he be overwhelmed by excessive sorrow" (2 Cor. 2:7). When God sends a storm, he expects the sailors to get to their tackling and do the best they can for themselves to keep the ship from going down. So we maintain our bodies as well as we can, and leave the degree of suffering to God. And what we do for ourselves, we should do also for our neighbor, with tender pity and compassion. The person who says that for love of another's soul he has no concern for his physical welfare falls under the rebuke of St. John, when he said, "He who does not love his brother whom he has seen, cannot love God whom he has not seen" (1 John 4:20). In the same way, the one who has no pity for the pain he can see in his neighbor will have little pity for the pain of his soul that he cannot see.

And sometimes God allows us to suffer that we might learn to pray to him for help. When St. Peter was in prison, the whole Church prayed without ceasing, and their prayers delivered him (Acts 12). When the disciples in the storm grew afraid, they prayed to Christ, saying "Save us Lord! We are perishing!" and at their prayer the storm ceased (Matt. 8:25). So it is in many cases: we call out to God in sickness and are made whole, or in dire weather and are brought through. We often forget our need for God in the midst of our wealth and happiness and we cease to pray, and God in his goodness draws us back to himself through suffering so that he can bring his graces to us.

XVI.

Concerning those who seek comfort, not from God,
but from the world, the flesh, or the devil.

VINCENT: This is a very good answer to my objections, uncle.

ANTHONY: Yet even so, cousin, there are many men who displease God in this matter. They abuse his goodness, and do not remember their Maker either in prosperity or in tribulation. When all goes well they forget God and follow their own pleasure; and when God graces them with suffering in order to draw them to himself, they grow angry and run from him, and go looking for help from any source but him. Some run to the flesh, some to the world, and some to the devil himself.

Consider the case of a man who has enjoyed good fortune, and has grown dull in his prosperity, wallowing in many sins that he finds pleasurable. God in his goodness sends him a remorseful conscience to bring him back. So the man begins to think about his past life, and then about his coming death. He realizes that he will soon leave all his worldly goods behind him and go forward alone to a place he does not know. Nor does he know when this might happen, or whom he might meet when he arrives. He considers that there might really be such creatures as devils, whose torments he had always thought nothing but tales of poets. If such thoughts as these sink deeply into him they will surely make him suffer; but if he takes hold of the grace offered by God, he will be consoled by remembering that God his father is calling him out of that far country of sin back home to the land that flows with milk and honey. And if he responds to that call, as many have done, how much joy will he then know! He will be glad to leave his wanton pleasures, do penance, and learn to spend his time on better things.

But let us take the case of another man who, when he is made sad by the call of God to his conscience, is very unwilling to leave his sinful pleasures behind, especially if it means that he will need seriously to alter his way of living to escape his sin, or make amends for his past wrongs to the great diminishing of his wealth. Such a man is in a sad state, for God continues to prick his conscience even in the midst of his refusal and his sins. He can find no happiness from either side. So he turns to his flesh for help, and does all he can to shake off his sad thoughts. He surrounds himself with physical comforts, fine clothes, and a soft bed, he distracts himself with witty conversation, and he runs after pleasures of the flesh with yet more energy. And at length, when he has behaved this way for a long time, God casts him off. Nothing is left but anxiety for the loss of his worldly pleasures and fear of his coming death. But when death approaches, he is again thrown into sorrow. No soft bed can help him then, and no human company can make him merry. There he lies, panting on his bed as if it were a pine bench. What a suffering it is then for him to remember his evil life, while his conscience convinces him of a coming heavy judgment! Then the devil attacks him with despair, and fills his mind with pictures of hell that can no longer be taken for mere fables. Yet still he does not turn to God.

I have seen men in their last sickness prop themselves up in their beds and invite their comrades to play cards with them, gambling away their time to keep themselves distracted from thoughts of their own foul life, of heaven and hell and the peril of their souls. They have played their games until the pangs of their sickness pulled their heart out of their play and kept them from understanding the game. Then their fellow-gamblers have quietly slipped away and let them die. Only God knows what kind of game such men then found themselves playing. I pray that it might be a good one, but I fear the worst.

Some men act like King Saul who in their suffering go in search of the devil himself. Saul had been told by Samuel how he should behave, but he paid no attention and grew worse and worse. When he needed to know God's will through the prophets, he was given no answer; so he went instead to the devil by means of a witch. He then came to the kind of evil end that comes upon all who meddle with the devil: his army was defeated and he himself was slain (1 Sam. 28). There are many foolish people who refuse to consult wise physicians when they are sick, and instead seek the help of a so-called "wise-woman," who is more aptly termed a witch. She will give them all manner of silly remedies that can do them no good. They have more faith in their witches than they have in God.

So it is with those who do not call on God in their suffering, but who seek for their help and consolation elsewhere, in the flesh, or the world, or the fiend himself. In their folly they turn what God meant for their good to their harm. But those who seek God in their tribulation gain both comfort and profit for their souls.

XVII.

Yet another objection answered.

VINCENT: All this makes good sense, uncle. Yet I have still a doubt about one thing. I have kept you a long time already, and I will soon leave you to your rest; but I wonder if you might address this matter. My doubt is this: I see by your explanation that a man may possess worldly prosperity and still be in God's good graces, and that a man may be suffering tribulation and yet be in the devil's grip; that a man may please God both by patience in adversity and by gratitude in prosperity. But if that is so, it would seem that both prosperity and suffering may be a matter for virtue or for sin, a matter of damnation or of salvation, and that neither are good or bad of their own nature, but are only good or bad as they are taken by those who experience them. That being the case, I see no reason why pre-eminence should be given to suffering, or why there is more consolation in suffering than in prosperity. In fact, it would seem that prosperity in this case would be better. For if a man who experiences good fortune gains God's favor by giving thanks, he is also spared much trouble that the person who suffers undergoes. And besides that, he can pray at his ease, quietly and with alacrity; whereas the one who groans with grief has a hard time thinking about anything but his pain.

ANTHONY: Let us begin where you end, cousin. We are agreed that for the wicked man, it hardly matters whether he is in prosperity or tribulation, for his desire to pray will be hindered, either by his pain or by his pleasure. Yet there is this difference, that a man sometimes calls on God precisely because of his suffering, while his pleasure tends to draw his mind away from God even if he is somewhat good. I think that few can deny this if they are being honest. When there is great suffering, anyone who is not a dull beast or a desperate wretch will call on God with a full heart, since his pain has made him serious. But when we are wealthy and at our ease, while our tongue patters along with our prayers, good Lord, how many crazy paths does our mind wander along!

Still I agree that there is sometimes so much suffering, in sickness for example, that a man can hardly even say his morning prayers. But God does not require long prayers for those in such straits; it is enough that they lift their hearts to him without any words. Such prayer is more acceptable than the long prayers people so often say when are healthy. The martyrs in the grip of their agony made no long prayers; but one inch of prayer in the midst of their pain was worth a mile or more even of their own prayers from another time.

The example of this is found in Christ himself. Though there was not and could not be any prayer of his that was not incomparably excellent, yet not all his prayers were alike. It seems that those he prayed in his passion were the greatest. When he fell to the ground in agony in the garden of Gethsemane and his bloody sweat fell to the ground, and when he prayed upon the cross, first for the pardon of those who put him to so much pain, and then commending his soul to his Father in heaven, surely these, among all his prayers, are the most efficacious. This example leads us to see that no prayer in the midst of pleasure is as strong and effectual as prayer amid suffering.

But now to go on to your question as to why I give pre-eminence to consolation gained in tribulation rather than comfort that comes amid wealth with thanksgiving. The first point is this: when a man takes suffering patiently for God's sake and his will is conformed to God's will, God rewards the sufferer in proportion to his pain. This truth shows up often in Scripture. But I can remember no Scripture verse that says that God gave a reward to a rich man for the very reason that he was at ease and comfortable while on earth. So a man who suffers can take consolation from his hope that God will diminish his time in purgatory or increase his reward in heaven, while the man in prosperity has no such hope due simply to his wealth.

But there are other reasons why I put the consolations that come from tribulation above those that come with prosperity. First, as I have before explained, continual prosperity with no suffering is a token of a lost soul. So suffering brings this much consolation at least, that a man knows he is not in that perilous state. Second, Scripture often commends suffering as the occasion of merit. The book of Ecclesiastes says, "It is better to go to the house of mourning than to go to the house of feasting; for this is the end of all men, and the living will lay it to heart" (Eccles. 7:2). And further, "The heart of the wise is in the house of mourning, but the heart of fools in the house of mirth" (Eccles. 7:4).

In addition, tribulation tends to the growth of virtue. It was said by the ancients that virtue makes itself known in matters of difficulty. It requires more virtue to conform our will to that of God in times of tribulation than in times of plenty. The devil saw this when he spoke to our Lord about Job. He said that it was no marvel for Job to be reverent toward God considering how much God had done for him. He knew it would be much harder for Job to be so loving and grateful to God if he was thrown into adversity (Job 1). But there he miscalculated, for the patience of Job in his short time of suffering gained him much more favor from God and was more commended in Scripture than all the goodness of his long and prosperous life. Our Savior himself said that it is no great thing to be good to those who are good to us (Luke 6:33).

It is true that prosperity was promised to the children of Israel in the old law as a special gift of God, but this was to draw them to God with pleasant things, as we give cake to children to help them learn their lessons. For in spiritual matters the Israelites were like children. But St. Paul says that "the old law brought nothing to perfection" (Heb. 7:19). It was our Lord who brought the law to its perfection: "Woe to you that laugh now, for you shall mourn and weep." But "blessed are those who mourn, for they shall be comforted" (Matt. 5:4). And he said to his disciples, "You will weep and lament, but the world will rejoice; you will be sorrowful, but your sorrow will turn into joy" (John 16:20). It is thus clear from the Scripture that tribulation is as far above prosperity as the day is above the night.

XVIII.

Summary of the arguments.

THEREFORE good cousin, lest you be taken too long from your other duties, let us end this time of conversation with a few final observations. If we believe, with firm faith, that Scripture gives us true doctrine, we can only think of suffering as a gracious gift of God that he gives to his special friends. Scripture highly praises tribulation, and calls men to practice penance if they continue long without suffering. We are told that suffering helps to purge our past sins, preserves us from future sinning, causes us to love this world less, diminishes the pains of purgatory, and increases our final reward in heaven. Suffering is embraced by all the apostles, exhorted by Christ, and without it we cannot be his disciples and cannot find our way to heaven.

Whoever remembers all this will not complain when tribulation comes. Instead he will begin by enduring his suffering with patience, and become better by thinking himself worthy to suffer. Then he will remember that God allows his suffering for his own welfare, and he will be moved to gratitude. The grace of suffering will then increase, and he will find great consolation in it, as he considers that God is always near to those who are in trouble. As a result his consolation will diminish much of his pain. He will not look for vain consolations elsewhere, but he will put his trust in God and look to him for help, submitting his own will entirely to God's. He will remain in prayer, and will ask help from his friends and especially for the prayers of priests, as St. James instructs. He will make his confession in order to be pure and ready for his departure, and he will be glad to go to God. If we do all this, I will boldly say that we will never go even half an hour in the midst of our tribulation without God's comfort lightening our hearts.

And if it is God's will to take us home, then our suffering has done much more for us. I fear what will happen to the one who is reluctant to leave this world. It will be hard to welcome a man into heaven who goes there against his will, and who says to his Master who has come to fetch him, "Welcome, my Maker—whom I do not want to see!" But I cannot believe that the one who so loves God that he longs to go to him will be anything but very welcome, even if he should go before he has been well purified. "Love covers a multitude of sins" (1 Pet. 4:8), and "the one who trusts in God will not be disappointed" (Rom. 10:11). And Christ has said, "I will not cast out him who comes to me" (John 6:37). So let us not desire a long life. Let us live well while we can, since God has commanded it, but if by God's good pleasure it is time for us to leave this life, let us be glad for it and yearn to be with him. Then our hope of heaven will comfort us in sadness, and we will go from our brief momentary affliction to everlasting glory, to which, good cousin, I pray that God may bring us both!

VINCENT: My dear uncle, may God reward you! I will not trouble you any longer. I fear I have worn you out with my questioning, and you have been a fine example of the patience you speak of by bearing with my folly for so long. Yet I would very much like to speak of these matters further with you at some future time.

ANTHONY: Let that time be soon, cousin, while our talk is still fresh in my mind.

VINCENT: I intend to commit this good counsel firmly to my memory. And my prayer for you is that our Lord will send you the kind of consolation that he knows will be best.

ANTHONY: That is well said, cousin. I pray the same for you, and for all our other friends who are in such need of consolation, and for whom you have been consulting me.

VINCENT: I shall make good use of your counsel on their behalf, and I trust that it will bring them comfort. May God keep you!

ANTHONY: And you, my good cousin. Farewell!

BOOK II

The Second Conversation: On Temptation

INTRODUCTION

Vincent pays a second visit to Anthony.

VINCENT: It has been a comfort to me, good uncle, to hear from your people that your health has somewhat improved since we last met. After leaving you I was angry with myself, remembering how long we talked and how much labor my questions cost you. I should have been more attentive to your health, and I was anxious lest our time together had made you weaker. But I thank the Lord that you have become somewhat better.

ANTHONY: No, no, my good cousin, it costs me very little to talk away like that. A foolish old man is often as full of words as a garrulous woman. You know how the poets like to paint us: all the joy of an old fool's life is to sit and warm himself with a cup and a roasted crabapple, and drivel and drink and talk! But to speak more seriously, our conversation was a great consolation to me. Though we spoke much of sorrow and suffering, our thought was not most about the tribulation itself, but about the comfort that may come with it. So I am very glad that you are here to continue our talk.

VINCENT: Our conversation was a great comfort to me as well, uncle, and to many others to whom I passed on your excellent counsel. I am delighted to be able to continue. Only promise me that if in my eagerness to gain your wisdom I forget myself and tax your strength, you will send me on my way.

ANTHONY: To tell the truth, cousin, I was a little tired after our long conversation, and thinking later about it, I could have wished that we had had less of my sermons and more genuine talk. But I lay the blame entirely on myself. It reminded me of what once took place between a cloistered nun and her brother. She was very holy, and for a long time had lived in a strict convent without seeing him. He also was a devout fellow who had been away at a university where he had become a Doctor of Divinity. Once on a visit home he went to see his sister. She came to the grate, and they touched one another's fingertips, which was all one could do in that place. And right away the good nun began to speak at length to her brother of the wretchedness of the world, the frailty of the flesh, and the deceits of the devil. On and on she went, until at a certain point she grew impatient with him and said, "In good faith, brother, I am surprised that you, who are so learned in all the things of God, do not give to me, your own sister, unlearned as I am and seeing you so seldom, some good counsel or exhortation."

"The truth is," replied her brother, "that I am not able. You have held the field, and have said enough for us both!" So, cousin, I will take a different path with you, and expect that you will do half of the talking.

VINCENT: An amusing tale, uncle! But if you really force me to take half the conversation, I am afraid that it will not go so well with you as it did for one of your now deceased relatives. I'll not tell you her name; guess it if you can! Her husband had a friend with whom he spent a great deal of time, often even staying away at mealtimes. So once when the husband and wife were together visiting this friend, she complained to him that he made her husband so comfortable that he stayed away from home. Their friend was a cheerful man with a dry wit, and he responded, "The truth, Mistress, is that there is only one dish that keeps your husband at my table. If you serve him the same food, he will never stay away from you."

"What might that be?" she asked.

"Just this," he replied. "Your husband loves to talk, and when he sits with me, I let him have all the words."

"All the words?" she said. "Oh, I see. Well, I am content then. For he will indeed have all the words when he is with me, as he always has—but I will speak them all myself! He can then do what he wants with them. And rather than let him speak even half, I am happy to see him at your table rather than mine!"

ANTHONY: I know just who she was! A very merry woman!

VINCENT: And as good as she was merry! But though you find fault with me for not speaking enough, uncle, I was ashamed that I spoke so much, and that what I said was of so little worth. Yet I see that you are content if I boldly speak my folly, so I will ask whatever comes into my mind.

I.

Whether worldly recreation can be used to gain comfort amid suffering.

AND before we go further, good uncle, can we return to something we spoke about earlier? You had said that in the midst of our sufferings we should not seek comfort in any worldly amusement or pleasure. In thinking this over I found it somewhat hard. Telling a merry tale with a friend can delight a man's mind and restore his courage without any harm. I believe Solomon says that we should give wine to those who are sad so that they can forget their sorrow. And St. Thomas says that pleasant talking is a good virtue, *eutrapelia* he calls it, because it refreshes the mind and makes it quick and eager after the fatigue of study has made it dull.

ANTHONY: I had not forgotten the point you are raising, cousin, but I thought it unnecessary to advise people to do what they will certainly do on their own. Even you and I, speaking together about as serious a subject as one can imagine, have been trading funny stories and idle tales. The truth is that I am by nature more than half an idle talker. I wish I could refrain from the fault as easily as I can perceive it, but old fool that I am, I can hardly help myself. I did not want to be so partial to a personal fault as to praise it.

But if we first agree that God alone must be our chief consolation,

I would not dare to say that a measure of good, honest fun is always to be forbidden. Many wise men have allowed it in some cases, and it suits the condition of our fallen humanity. I am sure that if we were in the state God at first intended, we would find talking about heaven the most refreshing and enjoyable activity we could find. But our affection for heavenly life has grown so cold that talk of heaven is a source of weariness and a heavy burden for many of us. Even the dread of hell seems to interest us more. Have you ever noticed that people listen when a preacher speaks of the pains of hell, but as soon as he begins to talk of the joys of heaven they get restless and move away?

It is with the soul as with the body: Some people, whether by nature or by bad habit, get into such a state that they cannot take wholesome food or medicine unless it is given to them with something that is less good for them, and if we wish to help them, we must let them have the less good with the good. In one of his conferences, John Cassian tells the story of a certain monk who spoke so sweetly of heavenly things that many of his hearers, forgetting this world entirely, began to fall asleep. When the good Abba saw what was happening, he shifted tactics and said, "I will now tell you a funny story." At that they all woke up and began to pay attention, and after he had told them the story they were able to listen to talk of heaven for a while more. If the only way we can bear to hear of the joys of heaven is to intersperse our talk with a silly tale—as if heaven were a place of sadness!—there is nothing else to be done. We could wish it were different, but so it often is.

In any case, let us at least make the times of idle refreshment as short and seldom as we can. Let us take them as our sauce, but not as our meat. And let us ask God for the grace to find such delight in the things of heaven that mere worldly recreation is almost a grief to us. If once we gain the grace to arrive at that point, we can be sure, cousin, that half an hour of the thought of heaven will bring us more comfort than a year of worldly refreshment.

VINCENT: Thanks, uncle. I can agree with your treatment of this question, and join you in prayer for the grace you speak of. And now, if you would, let us return to our main subject.

II.

Concerning the shortness of life in sickness or old age.

ANTHONY: As I have thought about our subject since we last met, cousin, I see that it would require many days to adequately cover all that might be said. And I am very aware of the coming end of my life. I am like the flame of a candle, that sometimes burns so low that it seems to have gone out, and then will suddenly flame up again and give a bit of light, until at last it goes out entirely. I know that I am not going to be here much longer, and I count every day as my last. There is a proverb often spoken to repress the blindness of thoughtless youth, that says that one can find a young sheep for sale in the marketplace as easily as an old one. But there is this difference between young and old: a young person might die soon, but an old person can never live much longer. So I think it best to concentrate now on just a few matters. If God gives me more time, we can continue our talk as you might wish.

III.

Concerning the three kinds of tribulation.

IT seems then that suffering can be grouped into three kinds: either the suffering that a man purposely takes upon himself, or the suffering that he willingly suffers, or the suffering he that is unable to avoid. The third of these, trials that cannot be avoided such as sickness, imprisonment, loss of friends, or loss of wealth, we have already spoken about at length. I will also leave aside the first kind, since a man who has embraced suffering as penance for sin or in devotion to God does not need additional consolation; the grace that has led him to acts of penance will give him greater comfort than whatever pain he is experiencing. And he himself knows how much he can handle, and can regulate his trial accordingly. Whatever his sin may have been, it is a supreme consolation for him to remember the goodness and mercy of God that infinitely surpasses all the malice of our sins. Christ spread his arms out on the cross to receive any who would come to him. Even the crucified thief, who only looked for mercy when he was no longer able to sin, was accepted and was promised a feast in heaven.

IV.

An objection concerning those who repent on their deathbeds.

VINCENT: The consolation you speak of is indeed great, uncle. In fact it is so great that I wonder if it might make a man think that he can boldly sin until the end of his life, and then be saved like that thief.

ANTHONY: Sadly, cousin, there are many people who so abuse the goodness of God that the better he treats them, the worse they become. Such people, even if they are saved, will not receive the reward in heaven that they might have had if they had repented earlier. It is true that God will extend his mercy to anyone who comes to him, even at the last moment, as is told in the parable where those who were hired to work in the vineyard late in the evening received the same reward as those hired in the morning. But that is not a good basis for thinking that we can boldly sin without concern. We need to remember that no one could go to work in that vineyard unless he had been hired by the owner. A worker who had made plans to be hired late in the evening, and who determined to sleep through the morning and drink through the day, was hardly likely to be hired at all. He would only go to his bed without his supper.

The story was once told of a man who claimed that he would

do whatever he pleased through the whole of his life, and at his approaching death he would simply recite three words of repentance and so gain his salvation. While he was still a young man it happened that he was riding his horse over a broken bridge. As the horse faltered and began to fall, the man fought hard to regain control, but he quickly realized that he would be flung headlong down into the raging river. In his fear of falling and sudden dismay he yelled out, "Devil take me!" Such were the three words on his lips when he drowned, the talisman upon which he had hung all his hopes.

So let no one sin now in the hope of later grace, for grace comes only when God wills it, and a presumptuous state of mind may be the very thing that hinders the offer of repentance.

V.

Concerning those who say that penance is only superstition.

VINCENT: Your point is well taken, uncle. But on the other hand, there are some these days who tell us that we need not have any remorse for our sins at all. We only need to determine to do better in the future and entirely forget the past. They say that the only purpose of fasting or of other bodily afflictions is to tame the flesh when we feel it growing rebellious. They grant that fasting is useful for temperance, but as for the practice of fasting or giving alms or doing any other good work as reparation for our past sins—they call this a bald insult to the passion of Christ by which alone our sins are forgiven. They say further that those who do penance for their sins are trying to be their own christs by paying their own ransoms and saving their own souls. This kind of talk has led many in Germany to stop performing any penance, which they call superstitious folly. And as for sadness or weeping over past sins, they call it womanish childishness—though the women there, God be thanked, are now so man-like that they can sin just like men without any shame or weeping at all!

But uncle, I am not so surprised at this ever since I experienced the manner of their preaching. You may remember that I was in Saxony before Luther had gotten married and when religious men and women were still wearing their habits. I happened to hear one of those preachers, who had a reputation for goodness and austerity and not a little learning, and it was a remarkable effort. I seem to hear him still, his loud, sharp voice echoing in my ears. He spoke fiercely against fasting and all such works—he called them the inventions of men—and he strongly urged his hearers to keep the laws of Christ, and to let go of their childish penance in order to seek nothing but salvation through Christ's death. "For he is our justice, and our Savior, and has paid all the price for our deadly sins. He made full penance for us through his suffering on the cross; he washed us clean with water from his sweet side; and he brought us out of the devil's grip with his precious blood. Leave, therefore, leave, I beg you, all these inventions of men, your foolish Lenten fasts and your childish penances! Never cease being grateful to Christ, and never look to save yourselves! It is Christ's death, I tell you, that must save us all—Christ's death, I tell you again, and not our own deeds! Leave off your fasting, and lean on Christ alone, good Christian people, for the sake of his bitter passion!" So loud and shrill did he cry the name "Christ" in our ears, and with so much detail and pathos did he describe Christ's bitter sufferings with the sweat dropping down his cheeks, that I was amazed he did not make all the women cry, for he made my own hair stand up straight on my head! The people were so taken with this kind of preaching that they began to break all their fasts, not from weakness or rebelliousness at first, but almost from devotion, lest they take from Christ the merit of his bitter passion. But once they had swallowed that first point, they came later to endure and accept many things that would have led them to rise against the preacher in anger if he had begun by speaking of them.

ANTHONY: May God bring that man to a better mind, cousin, and may God keep all good folk from that kind of preacher. A single preacher like that abuses the name of Christ and his passion more than five hundred gamblers who use Christ's name when they swear at dice. Such preachers hide their errors by constantly speaking of Christ and his passion, leading their hearers to forget that it has always been the teaching of the Church that without Christ's passion all of our penance would not be worth a pea. They get people to think that we are trying to save ourselves by our own deeds without the death of Christ; whereas we insist that Christ's passion gains incomparably more for us than all our own deeds. But it is also Christ's good pleasure that we suffer with him. That is why he said that all who would be his disciples should take their crosses on their backs as he did, and with their crosses follow him.

If fasting is good only for taming our passions and for keeping us from sinning, what must we say of Moses, who spent forty days in fasting? I wish he had not been so wild a man that he needed such a strong remedy. And what of Elijah, and our Savior himself? It was Christ who first began the forty-day Lenten fast that the whole of Christendom has kept, and that those preachers call foolish. When King Ahab went about mourning in sackcloth and ashes, it was not for the taming of his passions. Nor was it for that reason that the king and people of Nineveh fasted and went in sackcloth at the preaching of Jonah. They did it as a penance for their sins, asking God to pity them and to withdraw his indignation from them. I doubt that the widow Anna, who spent so many years fasting and praying in the temple until the time when she saw Christ, was doing this in her great old age only to tame her flesh. And the same can be said of St. Paul, who fasted often. The Scripture is full of instances that show clearly that fasting is no invention of men, but was instituted by God himself for many reasons. And to prove that one man's fasting can aid another, our Savior said that there are demons that cannot be cast out "without prayer and fasting" (Mark 9:29). So I marvel that these preachers speak against fasting and other bodily penances.

Yet I marvel even more that they so dislike the sorrow a man should feel when thinking of his sins. The prophet said, "Rend your hearts and not your garments" (Joel 2:13). And David said that "a contrite and humbled heart,"—that is, a heart broken, torn, and laid underfoot by sorrow for sin—"you, Lord, will not despise" (Ps. 51:19). He said of his own contrition, "I wash my bed each night with my tears" (Ps. 6:7). But why do I need to cite just one or two passages? The Scripture is full of instances that make clear that God not only expects that we amend our lives to do better in the future, but also that we should weep and be sorry for the sins we have committed. All the Fathers of the Church have shared this view, that we must have sorrow and contrition for our sins.

VI.

Concerning the person who cannot be sorry for his sins in his heart.

VINCENT: To be honest, uncle, I find this a little hard, not because I disagree with you that we should be sorry for our sins, but because it is often so difficult for a man to be sorry for past sins even when he tries. Though he may be ready for God's sake to avoid sin in the future, not only does he often find it hard to weep for his past sins, but sometimes he can hardly help laughing when he remembers some of them. If sorrow and contrition are so necessary that there is no forgiveness without them, I think that there are many who are in a very dangerous state.

ANTHONY: I am afraid you are right, cousin; there are many in such a dangerous state. And the saints of old are stern against them on this point. Yet "God's mercy is upon all his works" (Ps. 145:9), and "he knows of what we are made, that we are dust" (Ps. 103:3). He has pity on us, and does not demand of us what we cannot do. Let the person who finds himself in this state at least give thanks to God that he is no worse, and that he has determined to do better. And just as St. Jerome said to those who were weeping for their sins, that they should rejoice in their sorrow, so I would counsel those who cannot be sad for their sins, that at least they should be sorry that they are not sorry!

Yet while I would want no one to despair, I would warn such a person that as long as his affection for his past sins remains, he should be wary and walk with a double fear. First, because his inability to have sorrow for his sins is a sign either of weak faith or dullness of mind. If we really believe in God, and consider his great majesty and our many sins, the dread of offending him should break our stony hearts, and the love of him should bring us to tears. And second, since affection for past sins shows a conscience that is not fully clean and pure, and because no unclean thing shall enter heaven, I can only think that his mind will need to be purified before he arrives there. I would therefore hand on the advice of Master Jean Gerson, and say that since men are made up of both body and soul, if we do not feel affliction of soul as a result of our sins, let us afflict our bodies all the more, so that the one may purify the other. I am sure that those who do so, especially if they add faithful prayer, will come in time to find their hard hearts softened by a wholesome sadness, and a heavenly joy along with it.

But as I said the other day, cousin, I have no wish to dispute with preachers who teach such doctrines. As far as my own poor intelligence can gather, holy Scripture is against them, along with the whole body of Christendom in every Christian place. Even the countries where they live disagreed with them until just yesterday, and all the Church Fathers and doctors and saints have disagreed with them. If these new preachers have only now discovered that the Scripture has been misunderstood for all these centuries, and that all the great saints of the tradition were wrong about it, then it is beyond me to begin to study such things anew! Yet I think it far more likely that these men are wrong in their thinking and deceived in their understanding, rather than that the whole of Christianity has been wrong from the beginning.

Nonetheless, if it should happen that they are right, and that they have found an easy road to heaven that demands no penance, let them make merry, and sit and eat and drink for our Savior's sake, and play cock-a-whoop and fill all their flagons at once, and let Christ's passion pay for their feast. I am not the one to envy their enjoyment. But I can counsel no one to take their road. In any case, remembering the topic of our conversation, such men as these do not take upon themselves any suffering, so we need not discuss the comfort they might find in it. So I will make an end of speaking about this kind of tribulation.

VII.

Of the tribulation that a person does not purposely take on, but willingly suffers.

VINCENT: Excellent, uncle; you have brought the question to a good conclusion. You had spoken of a third kind of suffering, the kind that you planned to speak of last. Can we go on that?

ANTHONY: Gladly, cousin. You mean the kind of trial that is suffered willingly, even though it was not at first chosen. And here we will make another distinction between two types of this suffering: namely, temptation and persecution. Though distinct, these two types of trial are connected. Our spiritual enemy, the devil, persecutes us by temptation, and tempts us through persecution; and both come as suffering to a good man. The devil uses temptation like a snare by which he tries to catch us, while persecution is his plain open battle. So as we proceed I will call the two types by these names: temptation I will call the devil's snare, and persecution I will call the devil's open fight.

VIII.

Concerning temptation in general.

THE truth is that it is almost impossible to speak of every kind of temptation. The devil has a thousand subtle snares, and as many poisoned darts in open battle. He tempts us by the world; he tempts us by our flesh; he tempts us through pleasure and through pain; he tempts us by our enemies, and he tempts us through our friends. Sometimes he makes our closest friends our worst enemies, as Christ once said, "your enemies will be members of your own household" (Matt. 10:36).

Yet in every type of temptation there is a great consolation: namely that the more we are tempted, the greater is our cause of joy. As St. James says, "Count it all joy when you encounter trials of various kinds" (James 1:2). This should not be surprising to us when we remember that the world is set up as a kind of wrestling match, with the people of God on one side, and a group of strong and clever wrestlers on the other—I mean the devil and his proud but accursed spirits. For it is not only against our flesh that we must contend. "Our warfare is not against flesh and blood," says St. Paul, "but against the powers and principalities, the world rulers of this present darkness, against the spiritual hosts of wickedness in the heavenly places" (Eph. 6:12).

God has prepared a crown of victory for anyone who overthrows his adversary; but those who will not fight can gain no crown. "Only those who contend according to the rules gain the prize," says St. Paul (2 Tim. 2:5). And St. Bernard asks how it is possible to wrestle for a prize if there is no challenger to provoke the fight? So it is a great comfort to every person who finds himself challenged and provoked by temptation. He sees that his time of battle has arrived, and unless he behaves like a coward or a fool, he has the prospect of gaining his eternal reward.

IX.

A special comfort in all kinds of temptation.

THERE is one inestimable consolation to be kept in mind, as long as our faith does not fail. We can be sure that as we engage in the battle, God is always ready to give us strength against the devil's power, and wisdom against the devil's snares. For "the Lord is my strength and my song, and he has become my salvation" (Ex. 15:2). Scripture tells us that "if any of you lacks wisdom, let him ask God, who gives to all men generously and without reproaching, and it will be given him" (James 1:5), so that we can perceive all the wiles of the enemy. And Scripture is full of instances where God has promised that when we contend against the devil either we will not fall, or, if we should stagger and fall through lack of faith, yet if we then call upon God, our fall will not seriously harm us. "The just man, though he fall, will not be harmed, for the Lord holds him in his hand" (Ps. 37:23). The Psalm gives us a promise of God's help against all temptation, where it says, "He who dwells in the shelter of the Most High, abides in the shadow of the Almighty" (Ps. 91:1). The person who practices faith and hope is the one who dwells with God, and God will never fail to defend him in every kind of temptation. What weapon of the devil can give us a deadly wound if the impenetrable hand of God stands between?

Remember the image that Christ himself used in Matthew's gospel: "Jerusalem, Jerusalem, who stones the prophets and kills those sent to you! How often I have wanted to gather you as a hen gathers her chicks, but you would not" (Matt. 23:37). What a consolation there is in these words! We see the tender affection of God, who like a loving hen goes after even those of his chicks who are willfully running away from him and are liable to be taken by the swooping buzzard. How much more will he protect those who come running toward him. "In the shadow of his wings I sing for joy," says the prophet (Ps. 63:8). Not only do we find protection, but under the cover of God's heavenly wings we encounter great happiness.

X.

Concerning the four kinds of temptations spoken of in Psalm 91.

IN the 91st psalm the prophet gives us a kind of guide for our protection. First he says that the Lord will be a shield around us; and then he speaks of four kinds of temptation: the terror of the night, the arrow that flies by day, the pestilence that stalks in darkness, and the destruction that wastes at noonday (Ps. 91:4–6). This will give us a good way of understanding the kinds of tribulation we are now speaking about.

The Psalmist says that "his faithfulness is a shield and buckler" (Ps. 91:4). The shield here is a guarantee of our protection. As St. Bernard says, it is wide at the top and narrow below, since it is made of Christ's divinity and humanity. It is not one of those little round shields that hardly protect a man's head; this shield covers the whole body. Nor is it like shields of this world, that defend one part of the body while leaving other parts open and vulnerable. This shield encloses us such that the enemy cannot get at us by any of the four kinds of attack that the prophet mentions. The shield is our Savior Christ himself.

XI.

Concerning the first temptation: "The terror of the night."

THE Psalm first says, "You will not fear the terror of the night." Scripture sometimes uses 'night' to mean suffering, as is written in Job: "God knows their evil works and he overturns them in the night, and they are crushed" (Job 34:25), meaning that God brings suffering upon them for their wickedness. And we know that night is by nature a time of fears. So I understand the "terrors of the night" to refer to the suffering that comes from being tempted to impatience as Job was tempted, either by the devil, or by others he uses as his instruments. This kind of suffering is fittingly called the night's terror for two other reasons. First, because the sufferer often does not know the cause of his trial, unlike those times when the devil tempts him openly to do something evil or to draw back from something good. A second cause is that our courage often fails us and our fear is doubled at night, because we imagine things to be much worse than they really are.

The deep darkness of this kind of tribulation leads those without faith and hope in God to fear greatly. If they had faith they would know that whatever danger may press upon them, it is far less than they might think, since at worst it cannot touch their souls, only their bodies. But we are inclined to be much more concerned for our bodies that we can see and upon which we spend so much of our time and delight in feeding and clothing, than we are for our souls, since we cannot see them apart from the spiritual understanding that comes through the eyes of faith. We think that the loss of our bodies is much worse than the loss of our souls. Yet Christ tells us not to fear those who can kill the body and can do no more, but instead to fear the one who can cast body and soul into everlasting fire. St. Paul tells us in numerous places that the body is but the outward clothing of the soul. When we take more thought for our bodily welfare than for our souls we are even more foolish than a person who would neglect to save his life because he was worried about preserving his old weather-stained coat. Yet our fears multiply in the darkness. You know how it is: a man who walks through a forest at night will be afraid of many things that he would pay no attention to in the daytime. In his night-time fear, every bush seems to be a thief ready to attack him.

I remember once as a young man when I was a soldier in the retinue of the king (God rest his soul), we were camped beyond Belgrade inside Turkish territory. About midnight a cry was raised in camp that the whole Turkish army was coming upon us in a sneak attack. We were all warned to hastily arm ourselves and get ready for battle. When we had gotten ourselves armed and ready, the scouts who had brought the news were examined more carefully by our captains concerning what they had seen. One said that by the glimmering of the moon he had seen the enemy army coming forward in good order in a straight line. The others, upon being examined, said that once the lead scout had spotted the enemy they thought it better to run back and give warning than to draw closer to the enemy's ranks. They thought they had seen the same ranks, though from a greater distance and imperfectly. So we kept watch all night long, listening carefully for their coming. Every minute someone would say, "Hush, be still! I think I hear something trampling." As a result many of us also thought that we had heard them. But when dawn came and we saw nothing, the scout went out again with some of the captains to the place where he had first spied the enemy. When they arrived at the spot they found that the great and fearsome army of attacking Turks had somehow turned into a long hedge, standing stone-still in the morning light.

So it is with the terrors of the night. In order to fill us with dread and to overwhelm our faith, the devil works on our imaginations to make us think that we have far more to fear than we really do. Often enough the lion we think we hear roaring away in the darkness turns out to be only a silly braying ass. The dangerous rock in the dark night at sea turns out to be only a mist. But for those who hope in God, whether it is a lion or an ass, a rock or a mist, they "will not fear the terror of the night," knowing that God's shield surrounds them.

XII.

On pusillanimity.

MUCH of this night terror comes from the fault of pusillanimity; that is, of the faint-heartedness by which a person fears what he should not fear. The pusillanimous person often runs away from something that would not have harmed him if he had not fled. And sometimes the same enemy who would have run away if only the person had stood fast, grows bolder and attacks when he sees him fleeing.

The first effect of this kind of faint-heartedness is to make a person impatient under suffering. It will often then drive him to an attitude of stubborn anger against God, and even to falling into blasphemy like the damned souls in hell. It also often keeps him from doing many good things that he would otherwise accomplish if he trusted in God's help. But the devil throws him into cowardice, and deceives him into thinking that he is being humble when he claims that he is unfit and unable to do the good that God has set before him.

All this night terror comes from the devil, who takes advantage of our faint-hearted trust in God. Those who are tempted this way need to lift up their hearts and call upon God for help, and by following the good counsel of spiritual-minded folk, cast away the cowardice that has come about through their own imaginations worked on by the devil. They need to remember the parable of the talents, where

the man who fearfully buried what had been given him in a handkerchief lost everything through his pusillanimity. Let us then live in the
good hope of God's help, and this night fear will not scare us at all.

XIII.

Concerning the daughter of pusillanimity:
the scrupulous conscience.

PUSILLANIMITY gives birth by the night's terror to a timorous daughter, a silly whining girl named scrupulosity. This girl is never idle; she is always occupied and busy, and she makes a good enough housemaid. Her mistress loves her and is gentle with her, and is either pleased with everything she does or is content to pardon what she does not do well. But the girl never ceases to cry and whine lest her mistress be angry with her and she be severely beaten. Do you think her mistress will be happy with this state of things? Surely not.

I knew a situation like this once. A very wise woman with a mild and gentle spirit had a maid with whom she was well content. But she so disliked the maid's constant fear of her displeasure that she was forced to say, "I don't know what ails this girl! I believe the elvish urchin thinks me some kind of devil. With these false fears of hers, I would be unwilling to have her in my house even if she were ten times as useful as she is."

This is the way a scrupulous person doubles the fear of everything that comes along, and often fears when there is no cause for fear at all. Where there is no sin the scrupulous person sees a venial sin, and where there is a venial sin he sees a mortal one. Yet he still falls into venial sins, for who cannot? Then he is afraid that he has never fully confessed, or is not truly contrite and his sins have never really been forgiven. So he confesses the same sins over and over, burdening both himself and his confessor. He is unsatisfied with every prayer he prays, and prays it a second time, and then a third. His heart is left sad and fearful, and he is full of doubt and dullness and without any spiritual consolation.

The devil troubles many good people with this kind of night terror, trying to bring about some great evil. If he can, he will so fill a person's mind with the fear of God's justice that he will drive the remembrance of God's mercy right out of his head, and bring great weariness to his life. Further, by leading a person to take as a sin what is not a sin, or take as a mortal sin what is only a venial one, the devil hopes to get him to despair of forgiveness and actually to commit serious sins. Then, having made all the person's good works and spiritual exercises tedious and burdensome, the devil will subtly suggest a false doctrine of spiritual liberty as a way of release. When that happens the person's conscience will become as wide and easy as it was formerly narrow and straight. And after all, it is better for a conscience to be a little too narrow than a little too wide.

When I was a little boy, my mother had a good old woman that helped with the children. They called her Mother Maude. Have you ever heard of her?

VINCENT: Yes; I have heard much about her.

ANTHONY: Mother Maude used to take care of us, and would often regale us by the fire with childish tales. She once told us a story about an ass, a wolf, and a fox. The ass and the wolf both came to the sly wise fox for confession. The ass was all in a hurry and went to confession two days before Ash Wednesday, while the wolf would not come to confession until after Palm Sunday, and even then he put it off until Good Friday.

The fox asked the ass why he came so early to confession, even before Lent began. The poor beast told him that he was in great fear of his many deadly sins, and he wanted to be sure not to lose any of the prayers offered by the priests during Lent for those who had gone to confession. Then he confessed the great sin that was giving him such a troubled conscience: he had once angered his master by braying loudly early in the morning and waking him from sleep. He had many other such trifling matters to confess, for everything was a deadly sin with him. The fox afterwards told his badger friend that the confession had been a long and weary business, and only good manners had kept him from leaving the confessional and sitting down to breakfast with a good fat goose. The fox told the ass that his sins were mainly trifles, which was true. The most weighty matter in the bunch had been a tendency to eat too much. So as his penance the fox told the ass not to harm any other beast through his greediness for food. He then advised him not worry any more, and to be on his way.

Good Mother Maude told us that when the wolf went to Father Reynard—the fox—for his Good Friday confession, the fox shook his beads at him, and asked him why he had come so late to confession.

"Fr. Reynard," said the wolf, "I have to tell you the truth. I did not want to come sooner for fear that you would hear what a glutton I have been and tell me that I had to fast some part of Lent."

"No, no," said Father Fox, "I am not so unreasonable as that; for I don't even fast myself. I will tell you, son, just between the two of us here in the confessional, that all this fasting is not a commandment of God, but only an invention of men. The priests make fools of their people by insisting that they fast, but they shall make no such fool of me. I have been eating meat all during Lent. But in order not to be an occasion of scandal, I do it secretly in my own chamber, out of sight of those weaker brethren whose consciences would be offended. I would advise you to do the same."

"Father Fox," said the wolf, "that is pretty much what I do, God be thanked. For when I take my meals, I only do so in the company of those who have strong consciences, and strong stomachs too."

"Well, then, all to the good," said Father Fox. But when, later in the confession, he heard that the wolf was such a ravenous eater that he entirely devoured other animals, and sometimes spent as much on one meal as would keep a poor man and his family in food for a week, he preached him a short sermon on temperance.

"As for the fact that you devour other beasts ravenously, I can find no fault with it, since you have been doing it so long that you can hardly change your ways, and therefore it would be foolish to suggest it—even against good conscience. After all, you must live, and devouring other animals is the only trade you know. But remember! Too much is too much, and I perceive by your confession that you have not practiced temperance. So here is your penance: for the next year you should not eat animals that are worth more than ten dollars, as close as your conscience can guess the price."

So the two animals went off to perform their penances. The ass was about to eat a bit of straw, but then he saw a sow with her piglets, and his conscience grew scrupulous, and he didn't take even so much as a nibble. Someone then brought him some food, but as he was about to eat it, again his scrupulous conscience got in the way. He thought that maybe if he ate it, some other animal would not be able to have it. So he ate nothing at all and was practically starving, until word came to his spiritual father, who sought him out and gave him better counsel. The ass then cast off his scruple, sat down to his meal, and was a good, honest ass for many a fair day.

The wolf, meanwhile, was growing hungry, and remembered that he should not eat an animal worth more than ten dollars. He came across two scrawny horses, one of which could hardly stand, and the other already dead and lying on the ground. He was about to make a meal of them when he saw a fat cow and a young calf in the neighboring field, a much more enticing meal. He reasoned with himself this way: "Look at me: I was about to break my penance and eat these scrawny horses: but when I look into my conscience I can see that I have no idea how much they might be worth. Being so weak, they are no doubt gentle riders, and so are probably worth lots of money. But that fat cow over there with its juicy calf, well, there are lots of cows in this country; I'm sure it isn't worth much, and the calf can't be worth even half of that. The two of them together are surely not worth above ten dollars, so I can eat them both and not break my penance." And so he did, without any scruple of conscience.

If such beasts could speak, as Mother Maude said they could, I don't doubt that some of them could tell a tale as wise as this one. By this child's parable we can see that, troublesome as a scrupulous conscience may be, it does less harm than one that is overly lax. The worst kind of all is the conscience a man frames for himself as he pleases, making it narrower or wider like a leather strap to serve his convenience, as that wily wolf did. Let the one with a scrupulous conscience learn the custom in use among physicians. When a doctor becomes sick, however learned he may be, he puts himself into the hands of a fellow doctor and does not trust himself to his own care.

In the same way, those whose consciences are troubling them should submit their judgment to a good man who can give them wise advice, especially in the sacrament of confession. God is very present in that sacrament, and will bring to mind the remembrance of his mercy. Then the shield of God will surround him, and he will no longer fear this night terror of scrupulosity, and his conscience will find rest.

XIV.

Concerning the temptation to take one's own life.

VINCENT: Very good, uncle. It seems to me you have covered these night terrors well.

ANTHONY: Yet there is one more that I had not thought of before: that is when the devil tempts a man to destroy himself.

VINCENT: That is indeed a strange kind of suffering, uncle. Some hold the opinion that once a man falls into that fancy he can never fully cast it off.

ANTHONY: Yes, cousin; though one reason why people think so is that they are trying to understand why any man would kill himself, and they see that those who do so have often struggled long with it. But there are many good men and women who have been tempted to it—sometimes for years—and yet, by grace and good advice, have withstood the temptation and have been delivered from it. And because their suffering is not known, it is not spoken of. Yet a terrible suffering it is.

VINCENT: Please say something more about this, uncle. And first explain this: you have spoken of the night terrors as bringing about the fear of pusillanimity; yet it seems to me that this temptation to take one's own life arises instead from courage and boldness. These people dare to put themselves to death by their own hands, an act from which most men shrink and flee; and we know from experience that many who take their own lives are people of great heart and bold courage.

ANTHONY: I am speaking of this temptation, cousin, only as it arises from pusillanimity. It is true that some are tempted to kill themselves through foolish pride, and some by anger, without any fear at all and glad to do it. For them there is no suffering involved, and therefore it does not come into the topic of our conversation. But if you think that none take this road by way of fear, you are mistaken. Some of those who seem the strongest and most courageous are under just this kind of fear.

VINCENT: I find it surprising that you say that those who kill themselves in pride or anger are not suffering, and therefore are not in need of comfort.

ANTHONY: Then let me explain myself with an example. I was given one only yesterday by some friends of mine from Vienna. It seems there was a rich widow who had a proud and malicious mind—the two vices tend to go together—who had gotten into a dispute with another man in the town. She went to a poor neighbor and promised him a large sum of money if he would come to her house early in the morning and cut off her head with an axe. He was then to convey the bloody axe to the house of the man with whom she was disputing, such that it would be thought that he had killed her in anger. She would then be taken for a martyr. She had further planned that another sum of money should be sent to Rome, and that things should be arranged with the Pope so that she might be canonized!

The poor neighbor agreed to do it, but he had no intention of fulfilling his promise. When he was slow in its performance the woman got hold of an axe herself and insisted that he should come to her house on a specific morning and do the deed. He came on the designated morning, but he had alerted others to the plot and had hid them such that they would hear him talking with her. When he had spoken with her about her plans, he made her lie down and he took up the axe. He felt the edge with his thumb, and then told the woman that it was not sharp enough and that he needed to sharpen it lest it put her in too much pain. The woman was sorely disappointed by his going away, and refusing to be put off any longer with deceitful delays, she hanged herself by her own hand.

VINCENT: How terribly tragic! I've never heard the like!

ANTHONY: Yet the person who related the story, I can tell you, is the most honest of men. In this case her temptation did not arise from fear, but from high malice and pride. She was so happy in making her plans that she was not suffering at all. As I said before, this sort of temptation brings no tribulation, and so is outside our topic of conversation, which is comfort amid suffering.

XV.

About a man who was inspired to take his life
by an illusion of the devil.

BUT lest you think that this example is just a false tale, let me remind you of yet another case that you have no doubt come across in Cassian's *Conferences*. He speaks of a holy man who was held in great esteem by all the monks who lived in the desert. The man received many revelations, and some of the monks were concerned that they might prove to be illusions of the devil, as indeed it turned out that they were. For the man was brought by the devil's subtle suggestions to the horrible point of killing himself. As I recall, the devil went about his work this way: he made the man believe that it was God's will that he take his life, and by that means go straight to heaven.

Such deeds are not done from courage and strength of heart, because true strength is always allied to prudence. And also because those who seem most courageous are often in fact led to the act through fear and pusillanimity. This type of case touches on our conversation, for this is a severe and perilous kind of suffering. The devil may have brought the man into some secret and shameful sin, and through that sin he led him to despair of gaining both the life of heaven and the praise of men.

A person suffering in such a case should be dealt with sweetly, and should be encouraged by tender words to trust in God's mercy.

He should be told that if only he does not despair, this fall of his will be a source of joy to him. He had stood in greater danger than he knew, and God, who loves him, has allowed him to fall into the devil's trap to help him know himself better. Just as God allowed his sin as a remedy for his pride, so now, if the man will put aside despair and take up fruitful penance, God will again set him on his feet, and strengthen him so much with his grace that for this one defeat the devil has dealt him, he will deal the devil a hundred.

He must be reminded of Mary Magdalene, of David, and especially of St. Peter, whose bold courage took a foul fall. Yet because Peter did not despair of God's mercy, but instead wept and called out for it, God again took him into high favor, as the Scripture and all Christendom will attest. And let some good and virtuous people go to this man for advice in matters of their own conscience. By this they will show him that they do not esteem him less, but even more than before, since they think him more knowledgeable about the devil's craftiness. This will help him to lift his courage out of the desperate shame he has experienced.

VINCENT: This last suggestion seems to me dangerous, uncle. Would it not lead him to take his own sin less seriously, and draw him into the very pride that first drove him to despair?

ANTHONY: That could happen. But if a wise physician has the man in hand, he will know that some medicines that are good at one time may put the patient in danger at another. So he will give him the proper medicine at the right time, and will not continue it beyond its good use. If a ship is in danger from Scylla, the fear of falling into Charybdis will not keep a wise captain from drawing away from the peril. Once he sees himself out of the one danger, he will address the next. So in this case: when a man is falling into despair toward suicide, the wise physician will strengthen his courage with words of good consolation. When he sees the man out of that peril, he will think of curing his other faults.

VINCENT: It seems to me, uncle, that people tempted by the devil fall into this unfortunate state of mind in more ways than one.

ANTHONY: Very true, cousin. The devil seizes the occasion as it comes. He tempts some to weariness after a great loss, and some to fear of bodily harm, and some to fear of worldly shame. I once knew a man with a good reputation who fell into a strange fancy that almost wore him away. He thought that he had lost his reputation and that everyone took him for a fool, which was not at all the case; he was thought to be wise and honest. I knew of two others who were afraid that they might kill themselves, but they could give no reason for it. They were not afflicted by loss or shame, and they did not wish to do it, but they still feared that they would. One of them even asked his friends to bind him so that he would not kill himself.

VINCENT: That is a very strange way to behave, uncle.

ANTHONY: True, cousin; yet I think there are many who are in the same state. As St. Peter said, "Your adversary the devil goes about as a roaring lion, seeking someone to devour" (1 Pet. 5:8). He carefully considers the state and condition of every person, not only as regards external circumstances (property, wealth, authority, fame, and popularity), but also their inner state—whether they are in health or sickness, lighthearted or downcast, courageous or timid. Then he suits his temptation to what he observes.

He tempts the lustful to licentiousness, the ill-tempered to anger, and the melancholic to despair. With some, after suggesting a horrible sin to their minds, he plays upon them by getting them to think that the sinful thought itself was so outrageous that they are now outside the forgiveness of God. Whereas there is no thought so horrible and abominable that, if only it is striven against, will not become a matter for great merit, and no sin at all.

Some, happening to hold a knife in their hands, will suddenly be taken with the idea of killing themselves, and be made greatly afraid by the thought. Some have not been able to throw the idea away, and have later miserably done the deed. But just as the energetic man needs to resist the devil's temptations toward lust with grace and wisdom, so the melancholy man must resist his temptations toward despair and dread.

VINCENT: What advice would you give to such a person, uncle?

ANTHONY: There are often two sources of the temptation in such cases, one physical, and one spiritual. So the person needs two kinds of help, from physicians of the body and physicians of the soul. If proper medicines or a change of diet can help him to overcome some of his despondency, let him undertake them. And let no one think it strange that I am advising a physical remedy for a spiritual suffering. Our bodies and souls are so closely joined together that a disturbance in one often brings about a disturbance in the other. Just as St. James advises those who are sick to go to the priest for help in both body and soul, so I would advise some men who are sick of soul, besides going to a spiritual physician, to go also for a physical remedy. As for spiritual counsel, the first thing to do is to go to confession so that the devil will not have power over the man due to his other sins.

VINCENT: I have heard some say that their temptation was even greater after they went to confession.

ANTHONY: I don't doubt that in some cases it is so; but this is only a sign that the confession is helping them, and that the devil is angry about it. Sometimes we see in Scripture that the devil was most troublesome to the person he had possessed when he saw that Christ was going to cast him out. But we need to be ready to endure this kind of temptation, unless we want to let the devil do whatever he wants with us out of fear of him, for he is angered by every good deed of ours.

In fighting the devil's temptation, a man has three things to do: he must resist, contemn, and ask for help. His resistance comes mainly from his reason, as he considers how foolish it would be to sin and to lose his everlasting happiness. Whatever pain he may be trying to avoid, it will not be so great as the pains of hell. He should also consider that most of his temptation is a fear that comes from his own false imagination. All the devils of hell can never drive a man to sin against his will; but his own foolish imagination may do what the devil cannot. It is a like a man walking upon a high bridge, who grows so afraid when he thinks of what might happen that he actually falls, while if he had fended off his imagined fears he would have been in no danger. If others are calling to him, "Look out! You're going to fall!" he may well fall under the influence of their anxiety; but if they look at him merrily and say, "There's nothing to be afraid of!"

he will pass over the bridge with no problem. He would not hesitate to run over the same bridge if it were only a foot above the ground, but his imagination plays tricks with him. The same thing happens in temptation. The devil shouts in the ear of the man's heart, "You're going to sin!" and makes the foolish fellow think that he won't be able to take a step without falling. Just as a soldier sometimes does better to flee from his enemy's traps, so a man under this kind of temptation should not always reason against it, but should cast it entirely out of his mind and not allow himself to think about it.

The second thing to do is to rid ourselves of these pestilential fancies by showering contempt upon the devil. Some people make the sign of the cross upon their hearts, and then they laugh at the devil and scorn him, and turn their minds to some other matter. When the devil sees how little attention they give him, he often draws entirely away. This is not only because his proud spirit cannot endure to be mocked, but also because he knows that if he keeps up the temptation without getting the person to sin he will be giving a great increase of merit to him.

The third thing a person must do under this temptation is ask God's help, praying for himself and requesting the prayers of others, especially of good priests at Holy Mass. Let him ask for prayers from his own guardian angel and from saints to whom he is devoted, and let him use the traditional litany of the kind used by St. Gregory the Great during the Roman plague. St. Bernard counsels us to request such prayers of angels and saints. Some say that we do not need their prayers, since prayers to Christ are enough; and some go further and say that it is dangerous to ask the intercession of saints and angels since it is not counseled in Scripture. With such as these I will not dispute here; let them avoid such prayers if they wish. But as for me,

I would rather go with the counsel of St. Bernard and trust myself to his company than to listen to those who find fault with his teaching.

Above all let every good man have recourse to God, and remembering the ground of our salvation—Christ's passion—ask to be kept from these foul temptations to despair. Many verses can be found in the Psalms as weapons against the devil's temptations, such as, "Let God arise, let his enemies be scattered, and let those who hate him flee before him" (Ps. 68:1). Praying such passages in the midst of temptation is pleasing to God and terrible to the devil. None are more terrible to him than the words our Savior used to drive him away: "Begone, Satan!" And none are more useful to us or more acceptable to God than the words our Savior taught us: "Lead us not into temptation, but deliver us from evil." I am sure that those who use such remedies will be surrounded by God's protection as by a shield, and will not need to fear these terrors of the night.

So much for the night's terrors; and I am glad to be done with them and so come back to the daylight and the "arrow that flies by day," because I think I have made a long enough night of it!

VINCENT: True, uncle; but though the night was long, we have not been sleeping through it, but have been kept well busy! Yet I now think that we should pause in our talking lest you keep yourself too long from your dinner.

ANTHONY: No need, cousin; I broke my fast just before you came. And I think you will find this night and this day like a winter day and a winter night. Just as winter has short days and long nights, so you will find that this long night of fears will give way to a short courageous day.

XVI.

*Concerning the second temptation: "the arrow that
flies by day."*

BY the arrow that flies by day, I understand the psalmist to mean
the arrow of pride; the temptation the devil brings, not in the night
of suffering and adversity which is too fearful for pride, but in the
daytime of prosperity when courage and pleasure abound. Yet the
worldly prosperity that makes a man so happy and that tempts him
to pride is only a very short winter day. We start from the low cold
ground, and then suddenly we are shot up into the air. Yet though we
fly very high, even before we are fully warmed, down we come to the
cold ground again. During that short time when we are flying high
aloft, good Lord how proud we are! buzzing like summer bumblebees that never think of their coming death in the winter. Shot from
the devil's bow, the arrow of pride pierces our hearts and sends our
self-regard as high as the clouds, where we sit on a rainbow and view
the world from a great height, and in regarding our glory we think
that all those other poor souls whom we once thought our equals are
nothing but silly little crawling ants.

But however high into the clouds the arrow of pride may fly, and
whatever transports of joy it may give to the man who is carried up
by it, let him remember that even the lightest arrow has a heavy iron
head, and soon it will come back down and land on the ground. And

sometimes it lands in the muck and the mire where pride turns to shame and all glory is gone.

The wise man speaks of this arrow in the fifth chapter of the book of Wisdom, where he says that those who pass this life in pride and vanity will find that they come to a bad end. "What good has our boasted wealth brought us? All those things have vanished like a shadow... as when an arrow is shot at a target, and the air, thus divided, comes together at once, so that no one knows its pathway. So we also, as soon as we were born, ceased to be, and we had no sign of virtue to show, but were consumed in our wickedness. Such things these sinners said in hell" (Wis. 5:8–9; 12–13).

Consider how different are the thoughts of the proud man and the devil about this arrow of pride. The proud man has no clear target at which he is shooting; like a child playing with bows and arrows he shoots straight into the air to see how high the arrow can go. But the devil is shooting the arrow with a very certain target in mind. No matter how high it flies, taking the proud heart with it, he intends to have them both come down to the very pit of hell. He knows well from his own experience how the high arrow of pride never fails to fall, unless it is stopped by the grace of God along the way. When he himself was in heaven and began to fly high in his pride, he said, "I will fly up above the stars and set my throne on the mountains of the north, and I will be like the Most High" (Is. 14:13). But long before he had gotten half as high as his heart desired, he was turned from a bright glorious angel into a dark deformed devil, and instead of flying upward he was thrown down into the deep dungeon of hell.

Now it may seem to you, cousin, that the temptation to this kind of pride does not involve suffering, and so is outside our present conversation.

VINCENT: I had been thinking that, uncle. Yet I did not say so, since whether or not it pertained to what we have been discussing, I found your thoughts good and worth hearing.

ANTHONY: Yet consider, cousin, that though prosperity may be contrary to suffering, many good men find the devil's temptation to pride a great trial, greater than those who have not experienced it would believe. Just as it is very hard to touch pitch and never defile your fingers, or to put flax into a fire and keep it from burning, or to hold a snake close to your body and not get stung, or to put young men and women together without the danger of lust, so it is hard for anyone who has great wealth, whether a man or a woman, to withstand the suggestions of the devil and the occasions to sin given by the world, and to keep themselves from the deadly danger of ambitious glory. And if once they do fall into it, a whole flood of bad things follow: arrogance of bearing, forgetfulness of the poor, disdainful behavior, rapacity, extortion, oppression, hatred, and cruelty.

Many good men in authority see the danger of this kind of pride and they suffer greatly in being tempted by it. Some of them grow so afraid that they fall into the night-terror of pusillanimity; they forget God's help in keeping them safe, and they leave undone much that they should have done. Some even abandon their place and seek their own ease and comfort in a life of quiet and contemplation, wrongly convincing themselves that they are being humble by doing so. God is not content with this way of acting.

It can indeed happen that a man realizes that wealth and authority are doing his soul harm, that he is unable to perform his office well, and that things are coming to ruin around him. In that case I would advise him to leave his place, whether a spiritual or a temporal position of authority, and not make things difficult for those in his care. But if a man sees that he can do his duty reasonably well, I would recommend that he put off his fear. It is good to have a moderate fear of sin; as St. Paul says, "He that is standing, let him take heed lest he fall" (1 Cor. 10:12). But too much fear is harmful, and shows lack of confidence in God's help. Let such a man temper his fear with good hope, and let him consider that since God has set him in that place, God will grant him the grace to do well in it—provided it was God who gave him the place, and that he did not gain it through buying his office.

Let the man in authority observe what the devil tempts him to, and then lean in the opposite direction. Let him not be harsh, but instead pity and comfort those being punished. Not that he should let every evildoer go free; but let him be sorry for the necessity of punishment, and if he finds signs of amendment, let him be merciful. There will always be enough desperate wretches upon whom justice can be done for the sake of an example. But let the man in authority think in his heart that every poor beggar is his equal.

VINCENT: That will be hard for him, uncle, when he sees himself in fine rich clothing and the beggar all rigged in his rags!

ANTHONY: Listen to this, cousin: Once there were two men who went about begging together. It happened that a wealthy man took one of them aside and invited him into his house. He clothed the fellow in the finest silk, and gave him a wallet filled with gold. But he told him that there was a catch to his newfound wealth: in a very short time he would be returned to his former penniless condition and go about again in his rags. If that beggar, so finely dressed, were to come across his earlier companion, would he not take the man for his friend and fellow? And would he not be the silliest kind of fool if he thought himself better because he happened to enjoy a few weeks of wealth?

VINCENT: Indeed he would, uncle; there is no real difference between the two.

ANTHONY: Yet the difference between the richest and the poorest man in this world is not even as great as that. Let the one who is highest look at the one who is lowest, and consider how they both came into the world. Then let him consider that no matter how wealthy he may be at the moment, in a little while—it may be a week—he will be on his way out again as poor as that beggar. I would think such a man more than mad if for a short span of wealthy living—it might even be a few days—he seriously thinks himself better than the beggar.

Even natural reason will get a man that far. But a Christian with the light of faith will go much further. He will not only consider his own coming into the world and his going out of it again; he will think about the dreadful judgment of God, the fearful pains of hell, and the inestimable joys of heaven. And he will consider that when he and this lowly beggar have both left the world, it may be that the beggar will be raised to a level of such high royalty that the man would give anything to be made his equal. If a person will think seriously about such matters, cousin, I am convinced that the flying arrow of pride will never wound his heart, nor lift him even a foot off the ground.

In order to consider these matters well, let a man go to confession often, and gain the counsel of a wise spiritual father. Let him set up a solitary place in his own home as far from noise and distraction as he can conveniently arrange, and let him go there from time to time, imagining as he does so that he is leaving the world and entering God's presence to give an account of his life. Let him kneel before an altar or an image of Christ's passion, believing himself to be in the presence of the invisible God, as indeed he is. Let him then open his heart to God, confess his faults, and pray for forgiveness. Let him remember all the benefits he has received and offer humble thanksgiving. Let him declare to God his struggles: the temptations of the devil, the suggestions of the flesh, and the occasions of sin he meets with in the world, especially from his worldly friends who can be many times worse than his mortal enemies in drawing him away from God. Let him be sorry for his weakness, his negligence and his sloth in resisting temptation, and his readiness to fall into sin. And let him ask our gracious God for strength against his weakness, to keep him from falling and, if he has fallen, to mercifully lift him up again and place him in a state of grace. Let him never doubt that God hears him and will gladly grant his prayers. Living by trust in God's faithful help, such a man will use his wealth and prosperity to good effect, and God's truth will so surround him with a shield of heavenly defense that he will not fear the devil's arrow of pride flying by day.

VINCENT: I find this counsel very good, uncle, and can only think that if those who experience prosperity take your advice they will do great good both to themselves and to others.

ANTHONY: May our Lord put these thoughts, and better than these, in the minds of any who may need it, cousin. Let me now touch briefly on the third temptation spoken of in the psalm, the "plague that prowls in the darkness." Then we will call for our dinner, and we will leave the last temptation, the "scourge that lays waste at mid-day," until this afternoon. And God willing we shall then have finished our talk.

VINCENT: Lord bless you, good uncle, for taking such pains with me. But please, don't keep yourself long from your dinner.

ANTHONY: No fear of that, cousin. I promise that this matter will be brief.

XVII.

Concerning the third temptation: "the pestilence that prowls in the darkness."

IN the Psalm we have been considering, the prophet goes on to speak about God's protection from the pestilence (*negotium*) that prowls in the darkness. This *negotium*, this "busyness" is here the name of the devil who constantly tempts people to do evil deeds. His time of temptation is the darkness. But you know that besides the pitch black night which is the deep darkness, there are two other times of darkness: one just before the morning brings light, and one just as the evening falls. In the same way there are two times of darkness in a man's soul: one before the light of grace has possessed his heart, and the other when the light of grace is dimming because he is running away from it. The devil prowls in these two times of darkness, and he brings whatever foolish people he can find to follow him into all manner of bumbling busyness.

He sets some to seek the pleasures of the flesh in eating, drinking, and other filthy delights. Some he sets to incessant seeking after worldly goods. Our Savior said of people like these who are caught by the devil and are prowling about in darkness, "He that walks in darkness does not know where he is going" (John 12:35). Such is indeed their state; they don't know where they are going. They walk around in circles as if lost in a maze, and when they think they are at the end of their "business" they find themselves again at the beginning. Is this not always the way with the feeding of fleshly desires? However full-fed they are when they go to bed, they are as hungry upon rising the next day as if they had never eaten. So it goes with the stomach, and so it goes with the parts below the stomach. And as for avarice, it acts like a fire: the more wood is piled on it, the brighter and more greedy is the blaze.

The maze along which these people so busily travel has a center, a middle place, into which they are sometimes suddenly conveyed when they thought they were still at the outer edges. That center is hell, and all the paths of the maze lead there, often more quickly than they realize. They may think they have taken only a few steps, and then suddenly they arrive at their sure destination. As the Scripture says, "They spend their days in prosperity, and in peace they go down to Sheol" (Job 21:13).

As to the greedy, St. Paul says, "Those who desire to be rich fall into temptation and the snare of the devil, and into many senseless and hurtful desires that plunge men into ruin and destruction" (1 Tim. 6:9). Here is the middle of that busy maze, the very snare of the devil, where they are caught and drowned even before they are aware of it. Remember the covetous rich man our Savior spoke of, who planned to pull down his barns and build new ones to hold all his crops. God said to him, "Fool, this very night your soul is required of you, and the things you have prepared, whose will they be?" (Luke 12:16–20). He fell suddenly into the deep center of this maze of busyness long before he thought he was anywhere near it.

Now I realize that those walking about in this busy maze do not think they are suffering from all their busyness. But many are nonetheless deeply weary of it; their pleasures are so few and so short, and their griefs are so great and so continual. It makes me think of a good man I knew who had a vain wife, and as he watched the pains she took to tightly bind her hair in order to give herself a large forehead, and tightly brace her body with corsets to make her waist appear slim (both of which cost her a good deal of suffering), all for the sake of a little foolish praise, he said to her, "Truly, madam, if God does not reward you with hell, he will do you a great wrong. You have a right to it, since you are taking such great pains to get there."

Those who are now languishing in hell can see how foolish it was to spend all their energy in running after so little pleasure at the cost of such great pain. They now cry out, "We grew weary of the way of wickedness!" (Wis. 5:13). Yet while they were walking along that road they would not rest, but kept running on in their weariness, putting themselves through more and more pain for a decreasing amount of childish pleasure, short and soon gone. I think that there are many people who might have bought heaven with only half of the suffering they endured to buy hell!

Yet while these busy worldly and fleshly folk are prowling around the devil's dark maze, their wits are so bewitched by the secret enchantments of the devil that they hardly realize the long and miserable weariness they are enduring, all for nothing. They do not perceive their own suffering, and so they are in no need of consolation. It is not for their sakes that I am speaking of this, unless it might be in hope of their gaining some good advice, and by God's grace seeing the true state of their foolish misery. But there are many good and virtuous people, standing in the daylight of grace, whom the devil busily tempts to such fleshly busyness. They know that they have been given a large share of this world's goods, and they fear that they are not in God's light at all, but are only prowling about in the darkness with the devil.

Just as good folk in authority can fear the devil's arrow of pride, so good people who are tempted to sensual sins and greed can be troubled by the fear of this prowling plague. To be in moderate fear is a good state, and guards against our thinking too lightly of such perils and thereby falling into them. But we should not fear the loss of God's favor as long as we do not act on the temptation. Our fight against it will win us a reward in heaven, especially if we not only flee the deeds themselves, but also the inner affection for them and, as far as possible, the occasions of them.

To the degree that this touches on sensual sins, the matter is plain enough. But in worldly business and the question of covetousness, matters are not so clear. When good people who happen upon wealth read the thundering threats that God speaks against the rich in Scripture they can be greatly troubled. Our Savior himself said, "It will be easier for a camel"—or as some say, a thick rope, for that is what "camelus" means in Greek—"to go through the eye of a needle, than for a rich man to enter the kingdom of God" (Mark 10:25). So it is no surprise that some devout people experience dread when wealth comes to them. Yet Scripture always distinguishes between the possession of wealth, which is not rebuked, and the disordered affection for wealth, which is the matter for concern. When St. Paul speaks of "those who want to be rich," he is not censuring the having, but rather the willful desire and affection to have, and the longing for it. Such longing will surely lead to sin, for what we long for we will stop at nothing to gain. But to show that riches themselves are not forbidden, the Psalmist says, "If riches grow, do not set your heart on them" (Ps. 62:11). And though our Savior spoke of how hard it was for the rich to enter heaven—almost impossible—yet he immediately added that God can get them in easily enough. For what is impossible to men is not impossible to God for whom "all things are possible." He made his meaning yet clearer when he said, "How hard it is for those who *trust* in their wealth to enter the kingdom of God" (Mark 10:24).

VINCENT: Thank God for that, uncle. If every rich man were in such danger, the world would be in a very difficult state.

ANTHONY: It would indeed, cousin; and I think that it is so in fact. I am afraid that there are very few people who do not earnestly desire to be rich. And of those who have the desire, there are very few who do not set their hearts and their wills upon gaining wealth.

VINCENT: That, I fear, is very true, uncle; yet I was about to speak of something different. I was going to say that I cannot see how anyone can be rich in our world without danger of damnation, given that there are so many poor folk in it. A wealthy person cannot help seeing multitudes of poor people who lack so much while he has the resources to meet their need. St. Ambrose once said that if a person dies from need when another has the means to meet the need, it might as well be called murder. It seems then that every wealthy person must be in constant fear of damnation as long as he keeps his wealth. While I can see that a rich man, like Abraham perhaps, might maintain God's favor when there were not many poor people around him, in a world like ours where there are many poor folk in every country, anyone who keeps hold of his wealth must have an inordinate affection for it, since he has not given it away to those in need. So it seems, uncle, that the consolation you are offering to good people who are wealthy and troubled by the thought of it can be of little help to them.

ANTHONY: It is a difficult matter to set forth good or evil in the abstract, without consulting the specific circumstances in each case. A medicine that is good at one time for one person may not be good at another time for someone else, as any good physician knows. To go into all the possible circumstances that might be pertinent to this topic would make for a long and tiresome business. But let me respond to one part of your concern in as few words as I can manage. Then we can go to dinner.

First, cousin, I agree that a person who is wealthy and who keeps all his wealth to himself has good reason to fear for his soul. Yet I am afraid that such people are the last to be afraid, and cannot be called good, since they are far from the law of charity and give little or no alms from their wealth. But we should consider here, not the state of a person who keeps all his wealth, but rather whether someone should fear damnation for keeping any significant part of it. If the simple possession of wealth puts us in danger of hell, then all priests should simply teach that doctrine. God has indeed invited men and women to follow him in that way, leaving everything for his sake in voluntary poverty as an expression of longing and desire for heavenly things. But he has not commanded it as necessary for their salvation. He does indeed say that "he who does not leave behind all that he has cannot be my disciple" (Luke 14:33), but in other places he makes clear what he means. For instance, when he says, "He who comes to me and does not hate his father, his mother, his wife, his children, his relations, yes even his very self, cannot be my disciple" (Luke 14:26), he shows that a person must love Christ so far above all his kin, and even above his own life, that for the love of Christ he would choose him above them all. Christ teaches us to love God above all things; and those who love things of this world contrary to the will of God show that they do not love God above them. But I find no commandment that says that it is unlawful to have wealth.

As our Savior says, in his Father's house there are many mansions (John 14:2), and we will be happy to be welcomed into the least of them. The Gospels seem to say that those who suffer poverty while on earth will enjoy a higher place in heaven than those who had wealth. Christ counsels rich people to buy heaven for themselves (in a certain sense) when he says: "Make friends for yourselves by means of unrighteous mammon, so that when it fails they may receive you into the eternal habitations" (Luke 16:9). Yet even though this is the case, it may still happen that a wealthy person may excel in some other virtue and so be raised high in heaven. The proof of this seems clear in the case of Lazarus and Abraham. I do not mention this in order to comfort those with riches who like to heap up their wealth; they are hardly so proud or obstinate as to resist exhortation in that quarter, and they do not need it! But rather I speak for those good people to whom God has granted a measure of wealth, and whom he has inspired with the desire of using it well, not giving it up all at once but keeping some of it. Let them not despair if they do not give all their riches away, something God has not commanded them to do, nor called them to by a special vocation.

Zacchaeus was one such. When he climbed up a tree to see our Savior, and Christ called to him, saying, "Zacchaeus, make haste and come down; for I must stay at your house today" (Luke 19:5). Zacchaeus was very glad, and was touched inwardly with a special grace. All the people were scandalized that Christ would call to him and be so familiar with him, and they murmured against it. They knew him to be the chief of the tax collectors, a man who had grown wealthy through rapine, extortion and bribery. In their bold and blind judgment, they considered him very sinful and worth nothing. Yet an inward change was wrought in his heart that they could not see. Zacchaeus proved himself to have gone from evil to good. He received Christ gladly, and said, "Behold, Lord, the half of my goods I give to the poor; and if I have defrauded anyone of anything, I restore it fourfold" (Luke 19:8).

VINCENT: A gracious act indeed, uncle. Yet I wonder why Zacchaeus put things in that order. Should he not first have spoken of restitution, and only then of giving alms? For restitution is a duty based on justice, whereas almsgiving is a voluntary act. Zacchaeus would have spoken more fittingly if he had first made restitution, and then given half of what was left in alms. For only the portion that was left might justly be called his own.

ANTHONY: Fair enough, cousin, in the case of a person who does not have enough to suffice for both. But for the one who does, he is not bound to leave the poor without alms until he has tracked down all his creditors and paid them off. After all, many of them may be far away, and in leaving one good deed undone while he attempts the other, his good intention may fail and he may do neither. It is always preferable to do a good deed while we are still thinking of it. We will receive more grace, and we will be more likely to complete our further intentions.

But to come to the point: Zacchaeus promised neither to give away everything he had, nor to leave his office. For though he had misused his office before, he might hope in future to gain an honest livelihood by following the counsel of the Baptist, "Take no more than is appointed for you" (Luke 3:13). And our Lord, approving his good purpose and demanding nothing more than what he had promised, said, "Today, salvation has come to this house, for this one too is a son of Abraham" (Luke 19:9).

But I haven't forgotten your main point, cousin. You conceded in theory that a man may be wealthy and still be in God's favor, but you thought that in our time and place, with so many poor people about, no one can keep his wealth with a good conscience. Yet if that is true now, still I doubt that there has ever been a time when a man could be rich without danger of damnation. Since Christ's days to the world's end we have his own witness that the poor will always be with us (Matt. 26:11).

Yet there must be people of wealth in the world. If there were not, we would have even more beggars than we do. I consider this a sure conclusion: if all the money in the country were brought together tomorrow and put in a big pile and then divided equally to each person, things would be in a worse state the next day than they are now. It is in the nature of things that some men provide the means of livelihood for many others. Not everyone can own his own ship, or have a large inventory of goods. Not everyone can do a carpenter's job, or a mason's, or a tailor's. And where would the materials to build our homes or to make our clothing come from if there were no merchants? The rich man's substance is the spring of the poor man's living. Take away the one, and the other is reduced to begging. It would then fare for the poor man like that woman in Aesop's fable who owned a goose that laid a golden egg once a day. In her greed she thought to have a great many eggs all at once, and so killed the goose to get at the eggs. But she found only one or two inside the goose, and for her supposed gain she lost everything.

Now, cousin, let me address your doubt about how a rich man can keep his riches with so many poor folk in the world. We know that our Savior said, "Give to everyone who asks of you" (Luke 6:30), and if this were to be taken simply, the rich man would be obliged to give until the last penny was gone from his purse. Yet this saying needs interpretation, as St. Augustine has shown. He noted that while Christ said to give to all who ask, he did not say to give them all they ask. Yet if it is my duty to give something to everyone who asks, I will certainly be left with nothing.

It is similar to other commands of Christ: he tells us to love our enemies, to respond to evil with good, and not only to suffer injury with patience—whether the taking of our goods or harm to our bodies—but to give a good return to those who inflict the harm. Among these counsels he tells us to give to everyone who asks, meaning that if a man might perish if we do not help him, we should not refuse it even if he is our mortal enemy. But though I am bound to give something to every manner of man, friend or foe, who is in dire need, I am not bound to every person and to every case in the same way. Difference of circumstances changes the matter.

We need to provide for those who are in our charge, whether by nature or by law. By nature that means our children. By law, it means those whom we employ as servants. While our duties to these two sorts are not all alike, we are still bound to look after our servants, to provide for their needs, and see that they lack nothing while they are employed by us. If they should fall sick in our service, we cannot then turn them out of doors even if they can no longer provide the service we employed them for. That would be against all humanity. Yet more, even if a wayfarer should be received into my house, and become sick with no money to help him, I would consider myself bound to take care of him, and would not cast him out and thus endanger his life. It may be that God has sent him to me for just such a reason.

St. Paul says, "If anyone does not provide for his relatives, and especially for his own family, he has disowned the faith and is worse than an unbeliever" (1 Tim. 5:8). By God's commandment our parents are in our charge. Parents are to provide for their children, and both God and nature say that children should honor their parents and meet their necessities. Even in this case it may be that my father's need is so little and another's so great that I should meet the urgent necessity of the stranger—even my enemy, and God's too, the very Turk or Saracen—before I turn to the need of my father and mother. But apart from such extreme need, I am not bound to give to every person who asks money of me. Nor am I bound to believe every imposter that I meet in the street who tells me he is sick; nor to consider that all the poor of the world have been committed to my charge alone, and that no other man should give anything until I have emptied my pockets, as if God has left no good people on the earth except for me! I can think better of my neighbors and less well of myself than that, and still hope to come to heaven, by the grace of God.

VINCENT: Yes, uncle, but I think that there are some who would be very content to believe their neighbors so charitable that they can be at liberty to give the poor nothing at all.

ANTHONY: Too true, cousin; some will be content to think that way, or at least to pretend that they do. They are content to give nothing because they are nothing! But our concern is not with such as them, but with good people who fear offending God by keeping some of their wealth. I do indeed think that if a person holds onto his wealth for the sake of worldly splendor, delighting in it and liking himself for it, and thinking that whoever is poorer is far worse than himself, such a mind is caught by vain and foolish pride, and such a person is very wicked indeed. But on the other hand, there may be someone—would to God there were many!—who has no love of wealth, and when it falls to him takes no pleasure in it, and keeps himself in abstinence and penance as if he did not have it. He may outwardly keep up a good house and manage his affairs somewhat after the fashion of the world, lest he give occasion for others to wonder at him and take him for a hypocrite. But as between God and himself, like good Queen Esther he can testify that he has no interest in satisfying his own desires, and would as happily give up the possession of wealth, apart from the good he can do by keeping others in employment and running a household in good Christian order. If there is such a person, I think his possession of wealth may win as much merit as another's forsaking of wealth. At least it would be so if there were nothing beyond the mere forsaking of wealth that pleases God. But of course there are matters that please God that often go with the forsaking of wealth, like the fervent contemplation that so pleased Christ when he made Mary's part the better. Otherwise he would have been happier to see her busy helping her sister Martha, instead of taking a stool and sitting at her ease doing nothing.

But what about the person who has many possessions, but is not of so perfect a mind as I have been describing. He enjoys his wealth to some degree and has not fully determined in good Christian fashion to abandon the pursuit of pleasure. Well, what shall we say about it? He is less perfect than I could wish, and maybe less perfect than he himself could wish; but it is easier to talk about perfection than to perform it. Yet for all that he is not in a state of damnation. He is like the person who forsakes everything for a life of holy consecration and has not been as purified from all worldly desires as he himself could want, and he often rues the fact. Many a man has abandoned a powerful worldly position only to find that he has to fight to keep himself from the desire of becoming the cellarer in a monastery kitchen. He wants something to rule, even if it is only other men's stomachs. But God is very merciful toward our imperfections if we know and acknowledge our weaknesses, dislike them, and try little by little to amend them. God will not cast off a person and throw him to the devil if he has a general purpose of pleasing him and is trying to do so as much as his frailty allows.

And so to make an end of this point—of this devil who prowls in the darkness: If there is a person who wants to serve and to please God, and would rather lose all his wealth than to commit some deadly sin, and if he would readily give his wealth away without a grudge or a murmur should God so demand it of him, and if he would be glad to use his riches according to God's mind and does what he can to learn how to perform his responsibilities diligently, then, though it is true that everyone should fear that all the good we do is a great deal too little—such a man should dwell in the faithful hope of God's help. The truth of God will surround him like a shield, as the Psalmist says, and he will not need to fear the pestilence that prowls in the darkness, and by the great grace and mercy of God he will be welcomed into heaven.

AND here they come with our dinner. Now that we have finished the matter of our conversation I was about to send for it, but they have anticipated the request.

VINCENT: It seems that God is ordering both your conversation and your dinner, uncle! For the ending of your talk and the beginning of your dinner meet at just the right time.

ANTHONY: Let us then say our grace, cousin. And let us cease our talking for a time and see how well pleased we can be by our eating. After that—you know my customary manner, which is a bit impolite—I will not say farewell, I will only steal away for a little sleep. But I never sleep long in the afternoon; only briefly to forget the world for a space. Upon waking I will come and find you again. Then, God willing, the whole long day will be ours, and we will have more than time enough to finish the last remaining part of our conversation.

VINCENT: Please, uncle, keep your customary manner; it is polite enough. Just as it would be against good manners to expect a man to kneel as a courtesy when his knee is sore, so it is good manners that a man of your age, afflicted as you are with various illnesses that often do not allow you to sleep well, should take his sleep when he can. In the meantime, I too will leave you to perform a small errand, and then return to you again.

ANTHONY: Stay here as long as you wish, cousin, and when you have dined, go at your good pleasure. Only do not stay away long!

VINCENT: No fear of that, uncle. I have too much interest in taking up the rest of our talk.

BOOK III

The Third Conversation: On Persecution

INTRODUCTION

Vincent visits Anthony a third time.

VINCENT: I have tarried longer than I had planned, uncle, partly because I did not want to disturb your sleep, but especially because I was delayed by receiving a letter from Constantinople. It appears that the Great Turk is preparing a mighty army. No one knows just where he will attack, but I fear he is coming this way. It is said secretly in Constantinople that a large part of his army will be sent either to Sicily or to Naples.

ANTHONY: It may turn out, cousin, that this letter you received from your Venetian friend, though dated at Constantinople, was actually written in Venice. We have had letters from there before, and from Rome too, and other places, stuffed with tidings about some great exploit the Turk is about to accomplish. They broadcast these tidings only to further some affair of their own.

The Turk also has many men under arms, and unless he devises some way to move them around and put them to a project, they grow restive and difficult to manage. And he makes use of these constant maneuvers to keep those he intends to invade off their guard. For when they see that all this movement of war so often comes to nothing, they are then unprepared for the time when he actually attacks. In any case, cousin, I think it likely that the Turk *will* attack this realm of Hungary. There is no other country in Christendom more vulnerable to his attack, and there was never a time when he was more likely to succeed. For now we are calling him into this country ourselves—God save us!—the way the sheep in Aesop's tale invited the wolf into their pen to keep them from the dogs.

VINCENT: When that happens, uncle, all the sufferings that I first spoke to you about are sure to come upon us!

ANTHONY: Likely enough, cousin; but I do not think it will happen right away. Since the Turk is coming under the color of giving aid to one side against the other, he will bide his time before he shows his hand. But at the end of the day, even if he gains something for those calling him in, he will not fail to take it out of their hands again.

VINCENT: Yet they say, uncle, that he does not force any man to renounce his faith.

ANTHONY: Do they say so, cousin? Then they, whoever they are, are saying more than they can prove. The Sultan takes an oath on first coming into his office that he will do all he can to diminish the faith of Christ and spread the faith of Mohammed. It is true that he has not forced the people in every country he has conquered to renounce their faith at once. With some he is content simply to demand a yearly tribute of tax, and otherwise he lets them live as they wish. With some he takes nearly the whole population as slaves, and sends them across his empire with no hope of return. In some countries, especially those with large populations and developed cities, the number is too great to send away as slaves, so he removes the upper classes and gives their land and offices to others, either those he has brought with him or those among the conquered who willingly deny their faith for power, leaving the rest of the population little better than dead under their hands. In the rest, he allows almost no Christian to survive except merchants or those who serve him in war.

He handles the Christian countries that he conquers in various ways, whether making them into colonies such as Chios, Cyprus, and Crete, or bringing them entirely into his empire like Greece and Macedonia, and I suspect, like Hungary, if he can. The Christians are too many to sell as slaves, or to kill, unless he would leave the land desolate; and many—God be praised—keep their faith and are suffered to live in peace. But their peace is not very peaceful. They can own no land, nor can they hold any offices or practice any professions. They are taxed to the bone to support the Sultan's many wars, and their children are taken as youths and never see their families again. He forces some of the girls to become prostitutes, and some of the boys to be trained as soldiers. Others of the boys he makes eunuchs, not merely removing their stones as the old custom was, but cutting off their whole members. Many die that way, but what does he care? He has more than enough! And none of the children who are given as slaves to Turks or to renegade Christians are able to keep their faith. Their captors turn some of them to an evil end by using them as false accusers of faithful Christians, getting them to claim that they heard such-and-such a Christian man say something insulting about Mohammed. The falsely accused are then forced either to turn away from Christianity and become a follower of Mohammed, or they are put to death under cruel torture.

ST. THOMAS MORE

VINCENT: Good uncle, may our Lord in his mercy keep those wretches far away from here! I am afraid that if they come, many of our own folk will be ready enough to fall in with them. Just as a great storm at sea begins to roar before the worst winds come, so I hear that some among us, who just a few years ago could no more have accepted the name of Turk than that of the devil, now find little fault with them, and even begin to praise them where they can. And they are beginning to criticize all things in Christendom: its priests, its princes, its rites and ceremonies, its sacraments, laws, customs, and all.

ANTHONY: I think you are right, cousin. Things here in Hungary have not gone well since we found ourselves in political turmoil regarding the heir to the throne. And what is worse, some are inclining to the cause of the Turk, which they used to hold as abominable, as every Christian man and woman must. I also am gravely concerned by the open words spoken by many knaves in Hungary in favor of Mohammed's sect. Hungary has always been the key to Christendom. If once Hungary is lost to the Turks, a wide road will be opened into the rest of Christendom. Though he may not win it all in a week, the great part will be lost to him within a very few years.

VINCENT: But still I trust, good uncle, that Christ will not allow that sect of his mortal enemies to entirely prevail against Christian countries!

ANTHONY: Well said, cousin! Let us keep our hope securely in him, and we will not be deceived. We will gain either the thing we hope for, or something even better will come. The truth is that

I would have little fear of all these preparations by the Turks if we Christians lived as we should. And even as bad as we are, I have no doubt that this lowly Christendom will spring up again and continue up to the day of judgment, the tokens of which are not yet fully upon us. Yet before that time the Church will be hard put to it and will grow smaller, so small as to allow Christ to ask: "When the Son of Man comes again, will he find faith on earth?" (Luke 18:8). I don't think those end-times are yet upon us, so my view is that this ungracious sect of Mohammed will have a serious defeat, and Christendom will spring up and flower again. But I doubt that either of us will have the comfort and pleasure of seeing that happen. Our sinful living has brought judgment upon us, and God has allowed these infidels, his open professed enemies, to be the sorrowful scourge of correction upon evil Christians, who should be faithful but in fact are only his false friends. All this favorable talk about the religion of Mohammed is a sure sign of such falsity. Those who speak this way not only think that the Turks will come and rule, but they seem happy to live under that rule and to abandon the faith of Christ.

VINCENT: I go about more than you do, uncle, and I have heard much of that kind of talk. It was first a sort of jest, as men asked what it might be like to convert to the sect of Mohammed and so rule over other Christians and gain all their goods. But little by little it has turned from jesting to serious speaking.

ANTHONY: Though I do not go abroad often, I have heard similar things too, cousin. And though we should all pray that God keep his hand upon us and keep us from such wretchedness, I would ask every Christian man (and woman too) to consider that all this is very likely to come, and I would advise each person to sort out beforehand in his own mind, in the presence of God, how he will handle himself if the worst should happen.

I.

On the importance of preparing our hearts
in the face of persecution.

VINCENT: This counsel of yours seems very good, uncle. But I once heard a wise man say that it would be dangerous and foolish to imagine such a situation ahead of time, for two reasons. First, a person might determine that he would rather suffer any kind of painful death than forsake his faith, but afterwards fall into the fault of St. Peter, who made a proud promise and then had a foul fall. Or second, in thinking about the difficult things that are coming he might fall into great fear and decide ahead of time to forsake God rather than to deal with all that suffering. He would thus commit a grave sin in thought that he need not have committed, since the danger might never come.

ANTHONY: I have read similar counsels by good and learned men, cousin. Yet I would not advise anyone to follow such counsel. As to the first reason, though St. Peter said more than he could perform, this was no offense against God. His offence came not in his speaking, but in his lack of acting on what he said. Even if a man was never called on to act in such dire circumstances, it could not hurt him to go through life with a good purpose, like the poor beggar without a penny who considered that if ever he had great wealth he would give away much of it in alms.

But as to the second reason, that a man might forsake Christ in spirit before he was called to do it in practice, it seems to me that such a man has already so weak a habit of faith that the very act of putting the question will bring him more self-knowledge and may teach him the need to pray for greater grace and help. Besides, to counsel a man never to think about the worst that may happen is as reasonable as telling someone that the way to cure their toothache is never to think about the tail of a fox! How should he not think of it once it is suggested to him? That is an easier thing to command than to obey. And I think there are very few people who can escape thinking about the calamities that may come upon us, whether in private meditation or in company and conversation with others.

Most importantly, Christ spoke often and openly about the need to confess our faith even if others were to take us and drive us to deny him by the dread of death. It seems implied in this that Christians should be in the habit of keeping such a situation in mind, so that they can respond rightly if it should come about. If we find our hearts shrinking and our minds shuddering when we think about such things, we must call to mind the pain and torment that Christ suffered for us, and earnestly pray for strength to stand firm should such suffering come upon us. This kind of steady meditation seems to me the attitude that every Christian man and woman must cultivate, and that every priest should speak about with his parishioners even from the time of their tender youth, such that from their childhood on they calmly accustom their minds to it. Then the Holy Spirit will inspire by his grace a strong and habitual faith in them, and all the devils of hell with all their wrestling wiles will never be able to steal it from their hearts.

VINCENT: Your words ring true, uncle, and I wish I had thought about these matters sooner. But better late than never; may God give us the time we need to consider it all. And may you, uncle, continue with your good advice, so that we lose none of it.

ANTHONY: Gladly, cousin. There is only one temptation still to be considered, and I will go on to speak of it.

II.

Concerning the fourth temptation: "the noonday devil."

THE fourth temptation mentioned in the Psalm we have been discussing arises when we face plain and open persecution. It is spoken of as "the noonday devil." Of all the devil's temptations, it is the most dangerous, the most bitter, and the sharpest and most rigorous. In other temptations he works at night and uses pleasures to attract us and sets secret snares to catch us, or he comes at us during the day flying like an arrow, disguising himself so that we are blinded to his malice and can hardly see where he is or what he is doing. But in the open persecution of the faith he stands forth in the light of the sun—that is, he attacks even those who have the bright light of faith shining in their hearts—and he allows himself to be plainly seen, with all his malicious hatred of Christ and the Catholic faith. This is no wily temptation, but rather an invasion with furious force. In other temptations the devil sneaks around like a sly fox; but in the Turk's open persecution he assaults us like a roaring and rampant lion.

This is the most dangerous of all temptations. In other temptations the devil attempts either to flatter and give pleasure or to inflict suffering and produce impatience and sadness. But in this temptation he assails us both through the fear of pain and by the desire for retaining the good things of life. And the danger is increased because the suffering need not be endured. In other sufferings of pain or loss, our need is for patience and submission to God's will in the knowledge that something good will come. But in this temptation, when a man is held and threatened with evils but is promised freedom and even wealth if he will only forsake Christ and the faith, he faces the sternest of tests, since he need not suffer the persecution if he does not want to.

VINCENT: Given the great danger of this temptation, uncle, it is all the more important for us to be armed against it ahead of time by words of counsel and advice, the better to withstand it when it comes.

ANTHONY: Agreed, cousin. I suspect that you are somewhat more afraid of this temptation than I am, excusably too, given your youth and my great age. So let us proceed this way: you tell me the kinds of suffering you fear from this open persecution, and I will respond to each kind and will give you whatever advice and consolation my poor wit and learning can call to mind.

VINCENT: In good faith, uncle, I am afraid not only for myself, but for all those who are in my care—men, women, and children too.

ANTHONY: Yes, cousin, and I share that concern since your kinfolk are mine as well. The truth is that everyone has reason to fear this temptation both for himself and for others. Since God has made the welfare of our brothers part of our charge, no one with a spark of Christian charity can help taking thought for his friends, and even for his enemies. So let us consider not only the suffering that you or I may encounter, but the kinds of trials that may happen to anyone.

III.

On the loss of external things through persecution.

SINCE we are made of both body and soul, whatever can harm us must harm the one or the other, either directly or through what touches on their welfare. Let us consider first the loss of external things. What are we most likely to lose, and so by that loss to suffer pain?

VINCENT: We might lose money and possessions, career and position, and the ownership of lands for ourselves and our posterity. The loss of such things brings with it the pains of a needy poverty, the shame of begging, and sadness and heaviness of heart as we see our dear friends and other good and faithful people in the same condition, while evil wretches and infidels enjoy what we and our friends have lost. As for sufferings of the body, we would experience loss of liberty, forced labor, imprisonment, and a painful and shameful death.

ANTHONY: Your list is long enough, cousin. I fear that the loss of even a quarter of these things will make many people who now think that they would stand fast to stagger in their faith, and would lead some to fall away entirely. I pray that they may be brought to see their true state and be shown it like St. Peter, before the trial comes upon them.

But now, what kind of consolation can we provide against the terrible things you have mentioned? If these times were as fervent as in days past, a few words would do the job. In those times, the more bitter were the pains of persecution to be endured, the more fervent were the faithful to suffer them. And I am sure that anyone who had as deep a love of God as those martyrs of old, and as strong a longing to be with him and to see his glorious face, would be just as ready to endure such pain. But sadly, because of our fiery affection for our filthy flesh, we now have such a faint and feeble faith and so lukewarm a love of God that our desire for heaven is dulled, and the dread of bodily pain strikes all our devotion dead. It is therefore the more necessary for us to steadily think about these things and to develop a strong and deep-rooted habit of readiness to suffer for Christ's sake, and not behave like a reed ready to wave with every wind, or a rootless tree in a loose heap of light sand that will be blown down by one or two blasts.

IV.

Concerning the loss of the goods of fortune.

LET us then consider, cousin, these sources of terror and dread that the Turk raises against us, and submit them to reasoned thought. We shall then see that they are not to be feared or fled from as much as might seem at first sight.

To begin with external goods: these are neither the goods of the soul nor of the body; they are more properly called the goods of fortune, as they help toward our maintenance and comfort during the short season of our present life. I mean such things as wealth, honor, professional standing, and positions of authority.

We might ask: why does the world call these things good? What good do they really bring? What I mean is: if having strength makes a man strong, and possessing heat makes a man warm, and having virtue makes a man virtuous, how can these external things be truly called "goods," since the person who has them may often be worse rather than better—and as experience proves, more often worse than better? Why should a man rejoice in having what is most often possessed by the wickedest of men, as he sees every day? Does not the Turkish Sultan surpass all others of our day in possession of these very things? Yet how fragile they are! You will remember that some twenty years ago the Sultan of Syria carried himself as high as the Great Turk, but in one summer he lost his whole empire. Since great kingdoms and empires are so unlikely to stand, and are quickly passed from one man and people to another, what do you or I, or even the wealthiest person in the land, really have when we possess a pile of silver or gold? Nothing but white and yellow metal, less useful in itself than rude and rusty iron, except for a little glittering display.

V.

Concerning the insecurity of lands and possessions.

THERE are many people who prefer to possess their wealth in land rather than in money. They think that other possessions may be stolen, but their land will still be there forever. But what good does it do us that our land cannot be moved and will always be where it is, since we ourselves may be taken away and not allowed to come near it? What is the difference to us whether our wealth is movable or immovable, since we are so movable ourselves that we can be moved away from it? In fact sometimes there is more security in money than in land. If we are forced to flee, we may find a way to take some of our money with us, but we cannot carry away even an inch of our land.

If our land is really more secure than our money, why is it that in this coming persecution we are more afraid of losing our land than our money? When these two great empires—Greece in my time and Syria in yours—were conquered by the Turk, the land was lost before the money was found! If the whole physical world, cousin Vincent, were animated with a reasonable soul, as Plato thought, and had an understanding of the course of events, Lord, just think how the very ground would be laughing with scorn at that great lord, watching him build his palace and hearing him proudly boast that he and those of his blood were the lords and owners of the land! The ground would consider the matter and say to itself, "Oh you poor silly soul! You think yourself half a god, but in all of your glory are only a mere man dressed up in a fine gown! I have seen a hundred such "owners" as you, people whose names you have never even heard. Many of those who walked so proudly over my head are now lying in my belly. And there will be many more who will call themselves my owners after you, who will not be of your blood and who will never even have heard your name." I ask you, cousin, who owned your castle three thousand years ago?

VINCENT: Three thousand years ago! Uncle, no king, Christian or pagan, could answer such a question even if you cut it down to a third of that time, and cut that in half too. In much less time than three thousand years a plowman's family may be raised to a kingship, and a king's descendants may be left to pull carts. And the king will not know that he came from a cart, nor will the carter know that he came from a crown.

ANTHONY: Yes, cousin; there are many stories that have come down to us recording changes as wonderful as that, sometimes in the course of only a few years. Why then should we consider the loss of land such a tragedy when we see how insecurely we possess it?

VINCENT: Well, uncle, since it is such an advantage to possess lands and station, maybe the less secure the land is, the more unwilling we are to put it aside.

ANTHONY: Let me turn that argument against you, cousin. If the possession of a thing is insecure by its nature and is likely to produce fear on that account, it gives us less reason to love it, not more. And the less we love a thing, the less we should care if we were to lose it. Consider all the things we have been discussing: riches, a good name, honorable fame, and positions of authority. We love them and desire to possess them either because they are advantageous to us in this present life, or because they will gain us merit in the world to come by our proper use of them. Let us take the first case, where we love them for what they will gain us in this present life.

VI.

Concerning how little pleasure we gain from riches in this present life.

As for riches: we gain far less from them than our foolish imagination has us believing. I do not deny that wealth allows us to array ourselves splendidly in silk clothing—but wool is just as warm! Wealth allows us to feast on delicious foods of all kinds—but less exquisite dining without excess would be more wholesome! And the great labor required to gain wealth, the anxiety produced in maintaining it, and the pain that comes when we lose it, do more than offset whatever pleasure or ease they bring.

Just consider: wealth often robs its owner of his happiness and sometimes even of his life. Many men have been killed for their riches. And some deal with their ample wealth as if they only had a key to someone else's treasure chest. They live as misers all their lives rather than allow their hoard to be diminished. Some are so afraid of thieves stealing their treasure that they become their own thieves and steal it from themselves. They dare not let it lie in the open, so they put it in a pot and bury it in the ground where it lies until they die, and sometimes for many years afterward. If the pot had happened to be stolen five years before this person's death, he would not have known it or been poorer for it, since he never used it.

VII.

Concerning how little is gained by worldly fame.

LET us now further consider a good name and honorable fame. This may seem a worthy possession for a person to acquire. Yet here too I will insist that there is nothing in the nature of the thing itself that brings us any advantage. True, sometimes a good reputation or a famous name will cause someone to treat us better than he otherwise might. But by the same token, people of good reputation are often envied and hated by others who are thereby readier to do them harm.

As to the thing itself, what is fame but the puff of another man's mouth, something that is gone as soon as it is spoken? The one who sets his delight in the praise of others is feeding himself with the wind, and he will never be filled since there is so little substance in it. Such a man will often deceive himself about what others really think. He will believe that many are praising him who never speak a word about him; and even those who do speak of him do so far less often than he imagines. While one person is speaking well of him in one place, you can be sure that another is speaking against him somewhere else. There are many who will praise him to his face, but will laugh at him and mock him behind his back—and sometimes not just behind his back, but with subtle speech even in his own presence. Yet there are silly fools who have been so fed with this fond fancy of fame that they happily believe themselves to be praised everywhere, as if the world had nothing else to do but sing "*Sanctus, Sanctus, Sanctus*" about them day and night.

VIII.

On flattery.

SOME go so far into this pleasant frenzy of foolish vanity as to hire men to flatter them. Not only are they angry if another tells them the truth when they do wrong, but they are equally angry if their good deeds are not praised with enough warmth.

VINCENT: So true, uncle! Not long ago I witnessed an example of just this sort of thing, and I must stop you long enough to tell you about it.

ANTHONY: Please do, cousin; tell on.

VINCENT: When I was first in Germany, it happened that I gained the favor of an important churchman who was among the greatest landholders in that country. His wealth was such that it would have made him a great man in any country of Christendom. Yet he was vain beyond all bounds. That was a great pity, for it made him abuse many of the gifts God had given him. The man was never tired of hearing his own praise.

Well, one day he had given an oration to a large number of people, and he was so proud of his performance that all through dinner he was sitting on thorns until he could hear how those who were dining with him would commend him for his fine job. He sat musing with himself to find a clever way to bring the matter into the conversation. Finally, rather than letting the opportunity be lost, for lack of anything more subtle he bluntly brought the matter out and asked all of us who sat at the end of the table—for he sat alone in the middle of it—what we thought of his oration. After that, uncle, I can tell you that no one ate another morsel of food until it was completely answered, for they were all deep in thought as to how they might manage some kind of exquisite praise. They knew that anyone who presented a mere moderate commendation would be shamed forever. There were ten of us in a row, and one by one, from lowest to highest, we said our bit, as if we were in high council debating some solemn matter.

When my turn came, I'm not boasting here, uncle; with the help of our Lady I think I performed well enough. Especially so, in that being a foreigner, I had the opportunity to show my skill in the German tongue. I left Latin alone out of regard for the person who was to speak after me, who was an unlearned priest who knew no Latin at all, and I did not want him to feel himself outshone. But when that wily fox next to me came out with his commendation, he showed himself so practiced in the art of flattery that he left me completely in the dust. I saw then how skillful a man could become in the art of flattery if he spent all his time mastering that one craft. I made a silent vow to myself that if ever he and I were again matched at that table and were forced to produce flattery, I would flatter in Latin and leave him behind me. I am content enough to be outrun by a horse, but I will not allow myself to be outrun by an ass.

But here is where the game got interesting, uncle. The man who sat at the highest place and who was to speak last was a churchman with an important benefice, and also a very learned fellow in the

Church's laws. What a sight it was to see how carefully he listened to every word that was spoken before him! It seemed that the more proper and elegant were the words, the less he liked them, since he had to find a way to surpass them all. He was so anxious that he began to sweat, and more than once he had to wipe his face. By the time it was his turn to speak, the nine of us who had spoken before him had left him nothing to say.

ANTHONY: Poor fellow! Someone among you should have at least lent the good man one word!

VINCENT: As it happened, uncle, he didn't need our help. He found a way to surpass all of us with his flattery.

ANTHONY: Why what did he say, cousin?

VINCENT: By our Lady, uncle, not a word. He comported himself in the same way that Pliny records of the painter Apelles, who was painting the sacrifice and death of Iphigenia, and was putting sorrowful looks on the faces of the great men of Greece who were watching the deed. The last face he was to paint was that of her father Agamemnon. He needed to show the king's face as the most sorrowful of all, since no one could grieve more than the girl's own father. But when Apelles came to the king's countenance, he found that he had used so much skill in painting the other sorrowful faces that he could not come up with a yet more sorrowful face for the king, and that would have diminished the praise of the painting. So rather than showing the countenance of Agamemnon, he painted him holding his face in a handkerchief!

That was the ruse used by this honest flatterer at our table. When he saw that there was nothing more to be said, the sly fox would not speak a word. He gave a long sigh with an "Oh!" from the bottom of his heart as of one who had been ravished with wonder at the wisdom and eloquence of the oration. He then held up both his hands, lifted his head, and wept into his napkin.

ANTHONY: Ha! He played his part well, cousin. But tell me: was the great prelate's oration at all praiseworthy? You did hear it, true? You were not, I hope, like that blind senator spoken of in Juvenal, who sat praising a plate of fish at the table of Tiberius, nodding his head wisely and pointing at the wrong dish! I'm sure you would not have undertaken to praise the oration if you hadn't first heard it.

VINCENT: I did hear it, uncle, and it was well enough delivered. Yet it would have been justly served with less than half of the praise it received. Yet I am sure of this: if it had been the worst speech ever made, the praise of it would not have been lessened by a hair. Those who were in the habit of praising that great man never considered how much the thing deserved, but only how great a flattery they could concoct.

ANTHONY: Surely, cousin, as Terence once said, such men as these would make even a fool go mad. Their lords have good reason to be very angry with them.

VINCENT: God certainly has reason to be angry with them, and I daresay he is. But as for their lords, uncle, if they were to get angry at such men I think they would do them a great wrong. It is one of the reasons these vainglorious lords keep them nearby. They are much happier to have their behavior commended than amended. No matter how vigorously they may tell their servants and their friends to speak truth to them, you can be sure that they will be much better pleased by flattery than by truth. They are like that friend of the poet Martial who asked him to comment on some verses he had written, and insisted that he tell him the very truth. Martial responded with an epigram:

> "The very truth is what you require of me.
> The very truth, my dear friend, is just this:
> The very truth is what you would not be happy to hear."

The same prelate at whose table this game of flattery took place once drew up a treaty between his country and that of a neighboring prince. He thought he had devised the treaty so well and intelligently that the whole world would praise his accomplishment. Longing to hear some such approval, he called on a friend of his, an expert in these matters who had been an ambassador and had drawn up many treaties himself. The prelate gave him the treaty, and once it had been read, said to his friend, "Tell me how you like it; but I beg you, tell me the very truth." He spoke so earnestly that his friend thought he really wanted to hear the truth, so his friend pointed out an error in the treaty. At this the man swore at him in great anger, saying, "By the mass, you are a great fool!" The man told me later that he would never tell the truth to that fellow again.

ANTHONY: I can hardly blame him, cousin. Such vain people bring this on themselves. They make everyone mock, flatter, and deceive them. If they really wanted to hear the truth, they would do well to commend the people who speak truth to them and to withdraw their ears from flatterers. That would be more effective than saying twenty times how much they wanted to hear the truth, and yet get angry with those who brought it to them.

King Ladislav—Lord preserve his soul—used to handle his servants in just this way. When one among them praised a deed or a quality of his, if he saw that they were speaking what they thought was the truth, he would let it pass. But if he detected flattery in the praise, he would cut them off and say to them: "Good fellow, when you say grace at my table, never pray a *Gloria Patri* without bringing in the *sicut erat*. If you wish to praise me, always report it as it really was—*sicut erat*—and nothing besides. Do not lift me up with lies, for I do not love it." If others imitated that noble king, much of this false flattery would be diminished.

I do not doubt that it is a good practice to commend what is praiseworthy in others—always keeping our praise within the bounds of truth—as a way of imparting courage for the increase of such good things. Men, like children, are pricked by praise. But it is better still to do our work well and not to look for any praise. Of course the one who cannot find it in his heart to commend another man's excellence shows himself to be either envious or possessed of a cold and dull nature. But still, the one who puts his satisfaction in the praise of others is following a foolish fancy.

IX.

Concerning how little is gained in this world through positions of authority.

NOW what about the possession of authority that comes with high office? What is it that people most enjoy about authority? It is the pleasure of ruling and commanding others while living uncommanded and uncontrolled themselves. I was never aware of just how great a pleasure this was until a friend of ours told me the merry tale of how he had learned this lesson from his angry wife. When he evinced no desire for high office and would not work to get it, and when he even declined a good post when it was offered to him, his wife roundly berated him.

"Why will you not fight for office as other people do? Are you going to sit by the fire and make little geese in the ashes with your stick like children do? Would to God I were a man! What I would do then!"

"Well, wife," said her husband, "what would you do?"

"What indeed!" she said. "I would fight to the top with the best of them! As my mother used to say—God rest her soul!—it is always better to rule than to be ruled. By God, I would not be so foolish as to be ruled when I might rule."

"By heaven, wife," her husband replied, "in this I think you are telling the truth, for I have never found you willing to be ruled yet."

VINCENT: That was a masterful woman, uncle. And I suppose her attitude to be the same as all of those who seek positions of authority and hope to find pleasure in them.

ANTHONY: Yet I think there are few who find much pleasure in them once they have got them, cousin. There is only one person in a kingdom who can have such a high office as not to be commanded by another. No one stands in that position except the king himself. All the rest are under his rule, and most of them are under the command of others besides. Many men in high office have less control over their subordinates than their own commander has over them.

VINCENT: Yet it must please them, uncle, to see that others must salute them reverently and stand before them bareheaded, or even kneel in their presence.

ANTHONY: Well, cousin, to a great extent they are just playing a part: they receive reverence, but they must pay an equal amount to others. Twenty courtesies shown by others will give a man less pleasure than the amount of pain he experiences from one genuflection of his own to his superior, if his knee happens to be sore. I remember a man high in the king's service who once told me that twenty men standing bareheaded before him did not keep his head half so warm as his own cap. And all the pleasure he gained from having others honor him was not worth the pain that once came upon him when he developed a cough from standing bareheaded outdoors in the presence of the king.

But let us admit that there is some pleasure to be gained by holding high office. We still need to ask whether there are any pains joined with it, such that a man might do just as well in avoiding both as in having both. You know how hard it is to please everyone at once: in the same home the husband wants sunny weather to grow his corn while his wife wants rain for the sake of her leeks! Those in authority are never of one mind. They have their differences, whether for gaining profit, or in contending over power, or for getting favors for their special friends; and it cannot happen that both parties get their own way. And it is ten times harder for those in authority to see their will thwarted than it is for a poor man. This kind of thing happens not only to those in lower positions, but even to those in the very highest. Princes themselves cannot have everything their own way. How could they, since each one would be lord over the rest of them if he could? This leads to a great deal of private malice and envy of heart. Many will speak to a person in authority with praise and fair words, but if he should happen to have a fall, they will bark and bite like dogs to the attack.

There is also the cost and the danger of warfare, for which those in high office have more responsibility than the poor. Many a plain plowman can sit snugly by his fire while the holder of an office must rise and set himself to hard work. And then there is the easy change-ability of their state with every change of their master's mind. We see this happening almost daily. It is like the philosopher's parable, in which he compared servants of great princes to the tokens with which men reckon up their accounts. The token sometimes stands for a farthing, and then suddenly it is made to stand for a thousand pounds, and soon afterward it is again set for a farthing. It often fares that way with men who seek to increase their authority through the favor of a prince: they rise up high, and then they fall down again just as low.

And even if a man should escape all such difficulties, and maintain his office and authority until he dies, he must at last still leave his position. And what we call "at last" is a very short time. Let a man consider the years that it will take him to rise to high office, and then let him reckon the number of years he is likely to live in that state. I doubt that many who do so will have much reason to be happy. They will see that the time to enjoy honor and authority, even if nothing happens to threaten it, will be very short. And having once set their hearts on its possession, to be forced to leave it so soon will be a great sorrow to them.

So it seems to me, cousin, that the gains of having offices of high authority are not many, and the losses are neither small nor few. There are so many ways by which an office can be lost, and in any case it cannot be held for very long, and parting from it will cause grief. Given all this, I cannot see any good reason why anyone should greatly desire it.

X.

Concerning the harm that comes to the soul
in desiring worldly goods.

So far we have been considering outward goods, gifts of fortune as they are called, only from the standpoint of what they provide to worldly-minded people. But if we consider the harm that comes to the souls of those who desire them for the pleasure or advantage they bring, we will perceive how much happier will be the person who loses them than the one who finds them.

Advantages of wealth and station are of their own nature neither bad nor good; they will be either the one or the other depending on the uses to which they are put. Yet when they are sought only for worldly gain, we can be sure that the devil will soon turn them from being indifferent to being very evil. Though they are in themselves neutral, the use of them can never be so, but must be determinately either good or bad. If a man does not desire such things for a clearly good purpose, he will inevitably use them for evil.

For example, take the person who longs for wealth, not to accomplish something genuinely good, but only for his own pleasure. St. Paul tells us what will happen: "Those who long to be rich will fall into temptation and the snare of the devil, and into many unprofitable desires that drown men in death and perdition" (1 Tim. 6:9). Scripture also says, "The one who gathers treasure shall be thrust into the snare of death" (Prov. 21:6). Those who want wealth for themselves seldom have a careful conscience in acquiring it, and they work to get it by any means they can find. And having once acquired it, they either become miserly and keep it all to themselves, or they spend it on pomp, pride, gluttony, and all kinds of other sins. Either way they walk a damnable road.

As for the desire of worldly fame and glory, this does the soul inestimable harm. The heart of such a person is set on what is immoderate and above its true station, and puffed up in pride with the help of false flatterers, this brittle person—so lately come from dust and so soon to be laid low and rotted back into dust—thinks himself a god upon the earth and sets forth to lord it over creation. This leads to battles between princes, accompanied by all kinds of trouble and the shedding of blood, as a king seeks to reign over five kingdoms when he cannot even rule one well. How many kingdoms does the Great Turk rule? Yet he wants still more. And those he already has, he orders badly; but he rules none so badly as he rules himself.

And positions of authority? Those who desire them for their worldly advantage alone never handle them well, but instead they abuse their authority and do great harm to others. They forget justice and pursue unjust causes for their friends. They keep their own people prosperous by oppressing the innocent and the weak. They enact the kinds of laws spoken of by an old philosopher, laws like cobwebs that catch little gnats and flies but are broken through by large bumblebees. The very laws that are meant as a shield to defend the innocent become in their hands a sword to wound them. And the deepest wound in all this bad business is the one that such office-holders inflict upon their own souls.

So you see, good cousin, that all these outward advantages that men call the goods of fortune, if sought for worldly advantage alone, will prove a great trial even during this earthly life. They will not bring any great comfort to the body, and they will lead to the destruction of the soul.

XI.

How losing our worldly goods through persecution can bring comfort.

VINCENT: I cannot doubt the truth of what you say, uncle. The matter is so clear that no man can reasonably deny it. Yet I think there are next to none who will admit it. I find no one who confesses that he desires riches, fame, or authority only for his worldly pleasure. Every man wants to seem as holy as a saint, and will therefore say that he wants these things, not for himself, but so that he can accomplish good through them.

ANTHONY: Very true, cousin; that is the way all men talk. Some do so with outright hypocrisy, and some think that their selfish desires are only a small part of their motivation. And there are some who are not aware of their own worldly desires at all. God sees them, though they do not. But now look at the effect of this coming persecution by the Turk. If he arranges matters such that those who forsake their faith will keep their wealth, and those who keep their faith will lose their wealth, then this persecution will make many things clear, like a lodestone that separates gold from lead. It will expose the hypocrites from the true-minded, and it will bring self-knowledge to those who think themselves better than they are. You know the ones I mean, those who are always talking as though they intend the best, and who keep their great wealth as if in store for some deed of generosity that never comes. This is one of the consolations of the coming persecution: that it will separate the wheat from the chaff. It will help those who mean well but who never act on their convictions to have a good and meritorious reason for losing their wealth. And for those who really do act from the desire to please God, it will be no grief to them to lose their worldly goods, since they are ready to part with all that they have at God's good pleasure, and prize their faith above every earthly treasure.

XII.

Another source of consolation for those persecuted by the Turk.

VINCENT: Yes, uncle, I can see that those who have already been despoiled by the Turk can find consolation in what you say, and so make a virtue of necessity. But for those who have not yet been put to the test, I am afraid that this temptation is a very dangerous trial for them. I don't think that there are many who will be willing to forsake all their goods out of loyalty to the faith.

ANTHONY: I have the same concern, cousin. And in the light of the coming persecution this will be seen more truly. No matter how virtuous such people may have appeared, and even flattered themselves to be, yet in the sight of God their hearts were not right. Yet I would still ask such a one, even one with great wealth to lose: "What keeps you, good sir, from being content to let go of all that you have, without even any deliberation, in the face of this kind of persecution?" Tell me, cousin, how would you answer that question on behalf of such a person?

VINCENT: Since you ask me, uncle, though I cannot be sure of another man's mind, I imagine he would say something like this. "I have a great deal to lose—my lands, my position, my inheritance—all of which the Turk will let me keep, and perhaps even give me more, if only I forsake Christ. And I might further say that I have the idea of secretly keeping to some part of the faith, and only giving up those things in Christianity that do not agree with Mohammed's law. I will honor that law and call Mohammed a prophet and I will serve the Turk in his wars against Christian kings. And then I can continue to praise Christ, and to call him a good man, and worship him too, and so not entirely forsake the faith."

ANTHONY: Nay, my good sir, (so I would respond), Christ has no need of your praise at such a price, as if you could serve both him and his enemy at the same time! He has given you fair warning in the words of St. Paul: "What has Christ to do with Belial; what fellowship is there between light and darkness?" (2 Cor. 6:14). And Christ himself has said that no man can serve two masters. Christ wants you believe all that he tells you, and obey all that he commands, and to stay away from all that he forbids, with no exceptions. Break one of his commandments and you break them all. Forsake one point of faith, and you forsake them all, and you will get no thanks from Christ for keeping the rest. If you begin setting up conditions with God—what you will do for him and what you will not do—you will find that you are only making an agreement with yourself, and Christ will be no part of the transaction.

I would say further that even if the Turk were to make such an arrangement with you as you have described (which, believe me, he won't), you can be sure that he would not leave matters there. Little by little he would make you deny Christ and take Mohammed in his place. But Christ will not take your service by halves; he will have you love him with all your heart, or not at all. As if to prepare you for just such a situation as you now find yourself in, he told you fifteen hundred years ago that he would receive no such half-hearted service when he said, "You cannot serve both God and money" (Matt. 6:24). Such a conclusion is clear for anyone who has faith; and if you haven't any faith, there is no need to discuss the matter, since you cannot forsake what you do not have.

But anyway, after you have done whatever the Turk has required of you against Christ to the harm of your soul, what guarantee do you have that he will keep any of his promises concerning your beloved wealth?

VINCENT: The only guarantee a man can have is the Turk's promised word, which a prince cannot break lest he put a stain upon his honor.

ANTHONY: I have known the Great Turk, and his father before him, to break many promises more significant than the one he has made to you. Who will then take hold of him and cast into his teeth the accusation that he has broken a promise? What does he care for words that he knows he will never hear? Not a whit, I can tell you.

If you were to come later and explain your grievance to him, you would find him as shameless as a friend of mine once found the Sultan of Syria. This man had given the Sultan a large sum of money for possession of a certain office. But the office had scarcely been given to him when the Sultan suddenly turned around and sold it to another of his own sect, and put the Hungarian out. The man came to him and humbly tried to remind him of the grant he had been given, saying that it been spoken with the Sultan's own mouth and signed by his own hand. With a grim countenance the Sultan answered him, "I will have you know, you good-for-nothing, that neither my mouth nor my hand will be my master. I will be lord and master over both of them, and whatever my mouth may say or my hand may write, I will remain free to do what I like, and ask neither of them permission. Now get out of my country, you knave!" Do you think, good sir, that the Sultan of Syria and the Great Turk will behave at all differently in this matter of keeping promises, seeing that they belong to the same false sect?

VINCENT: I suppose I must risk it, since it is the only guarantee I have.

ANTHONY: An imprudent risk indeed, to put your soul in danger of damnation for the sake of your bodily comfort, not even knowing whether you will be able to keep that! But let us ask a further question. Suppose you could be sure that the Great Turk would keep his promise. Are you sure even in that case that you could retain your wealth?

VINCENT: I think I would be able to retain it.

ANTHONY: What if I were to ask you, for how long?

VINCENT: How long? As long as I lived.

ANTHONY: Well, let's assume for the sake of argument that you are right. Still, no matter how much the Turk may favor you, he cannot make you a day younger. Here you are already fifty years old, and each day a little older. Within a short time you must lose everything in spite of his favor.

A Dialogue of Comfort Against Tribulation

VINCENT: Well, a man may still be very happy to know that he will not lack for anything while he lives.

ANTHONY: But are you certain that even if the Great Turk allows you your goods, there is no one else who can take them from you? Might he not lose this country again to the Christians, putting you in the same danger that you now face from him?

VINCENT: I think that if once he gets his hands on this country, he will not lose it again in our time.

ANTHONY: Likely enough. Though if he were to lose it after our time, there goes your children's inheritance away again! But even if he were never to lose it, do you suppose no one else could rob you of your wealth?

VINCENT: I do not see who could.

ANTHONY: Do you not? No one at all? Not God?

VINCENT: God? Well, of course. Who doubts that?

ANTHONY: Who indeed? I will tell you who: the one who doubts whether God even exists. The Psalmist makes clear that there are such men, when he says, "The fool says in his heart there is no God above" (Ps. 14:1). Even the most foolish of folk seldom admit this in words; but this does not keep them from saying it softly to themselves in their hearts. I am afraid there are many more such fools around than most people think. They would be much bolder to speak their thoughts

171

openly if they were not afraid of what others might do; they certainly have no fear of God. We must leave such people to themselves, people so frantically foolish as to think that there is no God, and yet so pathetically fearful of men that they continue to call themselves Christians, until God himself deals with them, whether by bringing them secretly to a better mind through his grace, or by dealing with them openly, but rather too late for them, in his terrible judgment.

But I would say to you, good sir: you count on the Great Turk to let you keep your wealth if only you forsake Christ, but you also know that by this act you greatly displease God who can take your wealth away from you again. Why should you be so unwise as to please the one and displease the other, and lose your soul into the bargain? And further, since you believe that God exists, you also know that the Great Turk can do nothing that God does not permit him to do, just as the devil could only do to Job what God had allowed him. Do you really think that if God has allowed the Turk to take your wealth so that you might please him by remaining faithful, he will allow you to keep enjoying your wealth if you so displease him by turning traitor? Do you really expect to gain any benefit or enjoyment whatever from all your worldly goods in such a case?

VINCENT: Well, God is generous and gracious, and though a man may offend him, God often allows him to live long and prosperously.

ANTHONY: Long? No, good sir, he allows that to no man. How can you speak of living long and prosperously when your whole life is so very short, and half or more of it has already been spent? Can you burn a short candle down halfway, and then somehow still make a long lasting flame with what is left?

There is no attitude in this world worse than that of a man who attempts to delight in anything that he has gained sinfully. That is the straight way to becoming bold in sin, and finally to falling into entire infidelity, believing that God neither sees nor cares what we do. As St. Augustine says, the longer God withholds his stroke of judgment, the sterner will be the stroke when it comes. So you can be very sure that if you displease God by the way you are getting or keeping your wealth, he will not allow your wealth to do you any good. Either he will take it away from you quickly, or he will allow you to keep it for a while longer to your own harm, and then when you least expect it he will take you away from all your goods.

When that happens, what a heap of heaviness will enter your heart, as you are forced suddenly to leave all your piled-up wealth in one place as your body is put into the ground in another place! Then comes the heaviest stroke of all, when you find yourself being driven down deep toward the center of the earth, into the fiery pit and dungeon of the devil of hell, to remain there in torment to the world's end and beyond! What possible enjoyment in this world— even were it to last a thousand years—could recompense the intolerable pain you will suffer in one year? Or even in one day, or an hour? See what a madness it is, that for the sake of a bit of pale pleasure for a few scant years through your worldly goods, you cast yourself body and soul into the everlasting fire of hell, where your torment will not be diminished by a day even after you have been there for a hundred thousand years. Our Lord confuted and confounded this kind of foolishness when he said, "What good does it do a man to gain the whole world and lose his soul?" (Matt. 16:26).

VINCENT: Good uncle, I see how very true this is, and I am no longer able to imagine reasons to think otherwise. So I would like to put off this part I am playing, and instead ask God for the grace to play the opposite part by my deeds. I pray that I may never forsake my faith, whether in heart or in speech, for any wealth of this wretched world.

XIII.

*Concerning the wise way
to secure riches.*

ANTHONY: I think, cousin, that when this persecution comes it will not only test men's hearts and allow them to see whether they are corrupt and greedy or possessed of a pure heart, but the very fear of persecution may teach them the same lesson ahead of time. This will be a great benefit to them if they have the intelligence to profit from it, for they can then find a secure hiding place for their treasure that the Turk's army will never find.

VINCENT: I can assure you uncle, that many people will eagerly try to find such secure places to hide their wealth. I have known some who thought they had hidden their money safely, digging deeply into the ground and burying it there, who came back later and found that someone had dug it up and carried it away.

ANTHONY: I have known some like that too. But what happened to them is no surprise; they should have known better. After all, they were warned ahead of time not to hide their money in such places by someone who knew well what would become of it.

VINCENT: That was very foolish of them! Did this same person tell them where they should hide it instead, in a place where it could not be found?

ANTHONY: Indeed he did! Otherwise he would have given them only half a piece of advice. He laid the whole thing out for them. He made clear that burying treasure in the ground was no way to safeguard it, since it would be dug up by thieves and hauled away.

VINCENT: But where did he say they should hide it? After all, thieves can find money in lots of places.

ANTHONY: He advised them to lay up treasures for themselves in heaven, since no thieves can arrive there unless they put aside their thieving and become true men. And he knew what he was talking about, for it was our Savior himself. You remember his words: "Do not lay up for yourselves treasures on earth, where moth and rust consume and where thieves break in and steal, but lay up for yourselves treasures in heaven, where neither moth nor rust consumes and where thieves do not break in and steal. For where your treasure is, there will your heart be also" (Matt. 6:19–21). After hearing these words, I hardly think we need any more advice, or any further consolation for the loss of our goods to the persecuting Turk. Our Lord tells us where our treasure will be secure: in the hands of the poor. If we give our money away to those in need, it will lie safe there, for who goes searching a poor man's wallet for money? When we give to the poor, we give to Christ himself. And where is the persecutor who is strong enough to take that wealth out of his hands?

VINCENT: As true as this is, uncle, it is still so hard for men to give up their goods in this way.

ANTHONY: Yes, and especially hard for those who never hear any good advice about their wealth, or who hear it, but listen to it as if it were an idle tale. Yet if we take these words of Christ not only into our ears but also into our hearts, and consider that this is not some poet's fable but the very word of God, we would be ashamed to find our hearts and minds as dull and weak as before. This sad state of ours, that the seed of God's word has so little root in us, shows us that the thorns, brambles, and briers of our worldly riches have grown up so thick and high in the soil of our hearts that they are strangling God's word. God is therefore being gracious to us when, like a good farmer, he brings his people into the field—for our persecutors are his people—to grub up with their hoes and their pitchforks all the wicked weeds and brambles of our earthly wealth and carry them far away from us, in order to allow the word of God to have room in our hearts and to open a glade where the warm sun of God's grace can shine in and make the seed grow. If we put our treasure in the earth of this world, our hearts will become like our treasure, made out of mud. But if we send our treasure to heaven, our hearts will be found there. And the greatest comfort anyone can have in the midst of suffering is to have his heart in heaven.

If our hearts were truly not in this world but in heaven, all the torments that the world could devise would give us no pain. Let us therefore send our hearts to heaven by sending our wealth there. We shall then find that the consolation of the Holy Spirit within us will mitigate, diminish, assuage, and quench the furious fervor of the tribulation God is allowing us to suffer for the gaining of merit.

Consider: What if someone knew that in a short time he would be driven out of his land and would be forced to flee to another place? Wouldn't we think such a person very foolish if he refused to part with his goods and send them ahead of him to the place where he knew he would be spending the rest of his life? It is even more foolish if we, not knowing how long we will even be in this world, refuse to part from our goods for a short time because we fear a little loss. We know that we will soon have to leave them behind anyway; and in the process we would be putting our eternal happiness in jeopardy.

VINCENT: It does seem to me, uncle, that these considerations of yours are a great consolation for the loss of worldly wealth, and I only hope for the grace to remember them.

XIV.

Christ's poverty a source of comfort and courage
in the face of worldly loss.

ANTHONY: With trust in God's help, cousin, much less than I have said would be more than enough comfort. But in these sad times Christian fervor has grown very faint. It has gone from hot to lukewarm, and from lukewarm almost to stone-cold. To get that fire burning again will require us to put a load of dry sticks on it and to blow frequently on the flame. And yet if a man has faith, there is one thing alone that will console him for the loss of all his goods, something we have not yet spoken of.

VINCENT: What thing is that, uncle?

ANTHONY: I mean calling to mind the poverty our Savior willingly endured for our sake. Imagine that there was a great king who had such a tender love for one of his servants that he left all his worldly wealth, put off his royalty, and became poor and needy to help him out of some danger. I do not doubt that such a servant would willingly lose whatever he had rather than shamefully forsake such a master. Think then of the great goodness of our Savior. He is the universal king of all the world, and could have used his power in any way he wished. Instead he lived among us in neediness and poverty all his life, and took upon himself neither authority nor worldly wealth, all in order to make us rich, we who were not even his servants, but his adversaries and his enemies. The remembrance of this great goodness alone will so move a true Christian man or woman that they will be happy for his sake to return to God all he ever lent them—let us recall that they have nothing of their own that he did not first lend them—rather than forsake him in so unkind a manner by renouncing their Christian faith.

To sum up all that we have been saying about the fear of losing our worldly goods, let us remember these important truths: how little comfort worldly goods bring; with what great labor they are gained; how short a time they remain in the possession of anyone who has them; how much pain is mingled with the pleasure of using them; what harm comes to the soul from love of them; what great loss is incurred by renouncing the faith in order to keep them; how much is gained if for Christ's sake we lose them; how much more profitable they are when given away than when used badly; and finally, what rank ingratitude it would be to forsake Christ on their behalf, after he forsook all the world and endured a painful and shameful death for our sakes. If we consider all these things and imprint them on our hearts, abiding in the hope of God's help, we can be sure that the truth of God will surround us like a shield, and we will not fear this noonday devil—the open persecution of the Turk—no matter what loss of our wretched worldly goods we may incur. By setting aside the short and meager pleasure they bring in this life, we will be everlastingly rewarded by God with heavenly wealth, and live in joyful glory.

XV.

Concerning the fear of bodily pain.

VINCENT: So far as these outward goods go, uncle, I believe you have settled the matter. No one can be sure of himself, or know what strength he will have or how faint and feeble he may be when things come to a head, so I can make no guarantee of my own good behavior, especially when I remember how St. Peter himself was suddenly weakened at a woman's word and forsook his master so soon after he had boldly spoken and fought for him. Yet I do really think—and I trust that God will preserve me—that if the Turk should threaten to take everything I had, even to the shirt on my back, unless I renounced Christ, and if he promised me that if only I would join his sect I would gain five times more than I had, I would not for a moment take a step away from my faith.

But I have to admit that when my mind goes from my goods to my very flesh, and I begin to think about the physical pains that might await me in this persecution, I tremble with fear.

ANTHONY: I am not surprised at that, cousin, and I do not think you should be dismayed by it. Just think of the great horror experienced by our Savior when he was facing his own passion. Yet even as you shrink from pain and death, your mind still possesses reason, and you will be able to master your fear. Though you will naturally want to run from a painful death, you will be moved and strengthened by meditating on Christ's agony. He himself will provide the grace to conform your will to his, just as he conformed his will to the Father's. You will experience the secret inward consolation of the Holy Spirit, as he was consoled by an angel. You will follow him as his true disciple, and you will ungrudgingly take up your cross of pain and suffering, and die for the truth along with him, and thereby reign with him, crowned with eternal glory.

I encourage you in this way so that you will know that just because a man feels horror of a painful death in his heart, it does not mean he is falling away from God. Many who experience such fear turn out better at persevering than others who feel no fear at all. God knows our hearts, and does not call every man to martyrdom. Knowing the weakness of some, knowing their good will and maybe even their good courage, he sees nonetheless that they would play the part of St. Peter if they were brought to the test. Rather than exposing them to the danger of eternal loss, he finds a way to keep them from such a test, whether by allowing them entirely to escape, or by sustaining them in prison, or by calling them home early. We cannot say ahead of time what way God will take with us.

But if we are true Christians, this much we can say: that if without any foolish bravado or bold and rash promises—without trusting in our own strength—we determine that we will not forsake our faith no matter what torments the devil may devise, we can be sure that God will never allow us to undergo more than we can endure, and that with the temptation he will provide a way of escape. "God is faithful, and he will not let you be tempted beyond your strength, but with the temptation will also provide the way of escape, that you may be able to endure it" (1 Cor. 10:13). So St. Paul says in Scripture, and we can be consoled by this true word of God.

Therefore, cousin, since God knows what will come upon us and we do not, let us stand firm with high hope in the determination to keep our faith amid whatever persecutions may come. If they do come, our settled purpose will help us to withstand them. And if we should happen to take a fall in some matter of faithfulness—which God forbid—we will be readier to be put back on our feet again. If by good fortune the Turks are kept out, we will have lost nothing by our determined purpose, and we will be all the readier to give pure thanks to God. Yet if we do not make these resolutions ahead of time, and we decide to forsake Christ for fear of worldly loss should the Turk demand it, then whether the Turk comes or not we will have removed ourselves from God and his help. How shamefaced we would be in the presence of God should it happen that the Turk never came, and we had renounced our faith due to a shameful and cowardly fear of something that never took place!

VINCENT: Thank you, dear uncle, for these words. They have indeed given me great comfort.

ANTHONY: I am very glad for that, cousin. But if what I have said is true, then give thanks to God and not to me, for the work is his, not mine. I cannot say any good thing apart from him; and all the good talk in the world does us no good at all unless the Holy Spirit works inwardly in our souls.

XVI.

On the comfort to be gained in slavery or captivity.

AND now that we have strengthened our courage, let us consider more calmly the physical sufferings you had earlier called the worst part of persecution. If I remember rightly, you spoke of slavery, imprisonment, and a shameful and painful death. Let us begin with slavery.

VINCENT: Please do, uncle, for I think that it is a grievous suffering to be carried far from home as slaves in a strange land.

ANTHONY: I do not deny that there is real suffering in it, cousin. But for my part I don't think it is half as grievous as it would be if my persecutors could drag me into an unknown country where God could not find me or make himself present to me! But seriously, if I find that being taken captive into a foreign land is a great grief to me, I think that the fault is mainly mine, since I know very well that God is no more present here than he is in that distant country. If my whole heart is set upon God and nothing else, what difference should it make whether they carry me there or leave me here? And if I am troubled by the idea that I am not living in my own country and on my own land, have I not beguiled my imagination into thinking that I am at home here? St. Paul tells us the opposite, that "here we have no permanent dwelling place, but we seek the one that is to come" (Heb. 13:14). No matter where we are in this world, we walk in it as wayfarers and pilgrims. If I am troubled by being somewhere I do not wish to be, the trouble comes from not setting my mind and heart on God. When I mend that fault, my grief will soon be eased.

As for the other kinds of suffering that come with captivity and slavery, I admit that they are many and great. But they seem much worse than they are because we consider our current liberty to be much more than it is. What is captivity, bondage, or slavery? It is the violent restraint of one man by another such that he must do whatever the other commands and may not do what pleases himself. If we should be taken by the Turk, we would lament the loss of our freedom; but in reality, who is ever so free that he can do whatever he wants? God himself has put restraints on us by his high commandments, and human laws add an even greater measure of restraint. And how often are men constrained to do all kinds of things in the course of business or labor? If we keep this in mind, it will greatly lessen the burden of captivity.

I have still not touched on the greatest bondage we all suffer, even those who boast most loudly of their freedom. I mean slavery to sin, a true bondage. "Everyone who commits sin is a slave of sin" said our Savior (John 8:34). If that is so, why is it such a troubling thing to be made a slave by the Turk, since by our sinning we have so willingly become slaves of the devil? Look carefully at the great number of vile things we do daily, as the devil drives us by means of our blind desires and we prove too weak to repel him. This slavery to the devil is worse than any merely human slavery. If we are taken into captivity, let us use it to remember how willingly we have enslaved ourselves to sin, and let that be a consolation to us, and so by God's providence turn our enslavement to our own merit and the remission of our sins. And if it is such a grief to us that our wills are thwarted in our captivity, let us take the advice of Seneca, who said, "If you wish to do nothing against your will, try to engage your will in all that you are forced to do, and so you will always do your own will."

VINCENT: That is easily said, uncle, but very hard to do.

ANTHONY: Our proud minds make everything that is good hard to do. Yet we should remember that if we patiently serve others for God's sake, we will have a reward from God himself. And if we call to mind the humility of our Savior Christ, who though he was almighty God "humbled himself and took the form of a slave" (Phil. 2:6), we should think ourselves nothing but ungrateful cads if for fear of having to endure an earthly slavery for a short time we forsook the one who delivered us from eternal slavery to the devil by his death, and who will exchange our short bondage for everlasting freedom.

VINCENT: That is very well said, uncle. And while no one would be happy to be taken captive and made a slave, yet you have helped me see that it is not so hard to bear as I had earlier thought. Could you go further and say something about the pain of imprisonment?

XVII.

On the comfort to be found when facing imprisonment.

ANTHONY: With a good will, cousin. Let us first consider what the nature of imprisonment is. Once we do that I think we will have less fear of it. Imprisonment then is simply a restraint upon our freedom such that we cannot go where we would like.

VINCENT: Yes, by St. Mary, uncle, but I think that hardly tells the tale. Besides hindering and restraining our freedom, there are many sharp sufferings associated with it.

ANTHONY: True, cousin; I hadn't forgotten those further trials. But first I want to consider imprisonment alone. For a man may be imprisoned and yet not be put in the stocks or collared around the neck, just as a man may be allowed to walk where he wishes and still have a pair of chains riveted to his legs. They have that practice in Spain and Portugal, you know, and in this country too, where all slaves go about in that manner. So let us first put aside the suffering that is accidental to imprisonment, the kind that a man may suffer even if he is not imprisoned, or not suffer even if he is. Afterwards we can go on to speak about such additional sufferings as you may wish to bring up.

VINCENT: I am sorry for my interruption, uncle. Your orderly way of dealing with the question is best; and I must say that even without all those additional sufferings, the simple fact of imprisonment is a very tedious thing, no matter how comfortable it might be. Even in such a case as when a Christian prince is taken in battle and made captive, and his enemy treats him with humanity and consideration—unlike these infidel emperors, by the way, who often treat their noble captives worse than the poorest soldier, as the Mongol emperor Tamerlane kept the Great Turk near him and used him as a footstool for mounting his horse—yet as I was saying, even if the captivity is gently handled and a man were allowed to wander in fair gardens instead of being kept in a narrow room, it would still seem to me a great grief for him to be restrained within prescribed limits and bounds, and to be unable to go where he might wish.

ANTHONY: That is well thought, cousin. It brings to mind a question I had wanted to ask you. If two men were kept in two different rooms of a large castle, one of the rooms being much more spacious than the other, would they both be prisoners, or would only the one in the small room be a prisoner?

VINCENT: How could they not both be prisoners, uncle, even if the one were chained tight in stocks and the other had the whole castle in which to roam?

ANTHONY: I agree, cousin. But if that is true, if imprisonment is the lack of freedom to go where we please, let me ask a further question. Of all the people you know, is there even one man among them who is not in prison?

VINCENT: Even one man, uncle? Rather, none of them! I don't think I know anyone who is a prisoner.

ANTHONY: Ah, so I see that you do not visit prisoners often, as our Savior directed us to do?

VINCENT: If the truth be told, uncle, and God be merciful to me, no. I sometimes send them alms, but I do not enjoy seeing men in such misery.

ANTHONY: Dear cousin Vincent, though I say it to your face, I insist that you have many good qualities. But I must also say to your face that this is not one of them. If you amend this fault, you will have one good quality more, or rather three or four, since there is no telling what good things will come to a man's soul who makes personal visits to poor prisoners in jail. But since you can name none of your acquaintance who is in prison, can you name some of those you know who are *not* in prison? For I must tell you that I know as few *out* of prison as you seem to know *in* prison.

VINCENT: That seems strange, uncle. Anyone who can go where he wishes is out of prison, even the poorest beggar in town. And from my point of view, a poor beggar who is free to go where he wants is in a better state than a king who is restrained in a prison.

ANTHONY: Well, cousin, we can consider that free beggar of yours in a moment. But as to that king, I can hardly see how a prince is anywhere but in prison. If by imprisonment is meant the lack of freedom to go where one wills, then the Great Turk himself is in prison, since he is not free to go wherever he wants. He'd very much like to go into Portugal, Italy, Spain, France, Germany, and England, and as far in the opposite direction too, all the way to the land of Prester John and China, but he cannot. Many beggars are freer to go wherever they wish than princes and kings, hemmed in as they are by their offices and their duties. Yet there are places where neither the beggar nor the king can freely go without others restraining them and telling them they have no permission. So if imprisonment is what you say it is, I cannot see how either of them is out of prison.

VINCENT: Yes, but uncle, both of them have room enough—the king on his own lands and the beggar on the lands of others and on common highways—such that they could grow weary from all their walking without anyone getting in their way.

ANTHONY: But the same could be said for that king we spoke about, who, as you put the case, had a whole castle to walk around in, and yet was still as much of a prisoner as the one kept in stocks.

VINCENT: Well, at least they can go everywhere they need to go or that is comfortable for them, and therefore they don't wish to go anywhere they can't go. So for all practical purposes they are free to go wherever they want.

ANTHONY: Yet still I would insist that every man is constrained, and cannot go wherever he wants, and therefore, according to our definition, is in prison. And I would further say that if we look at both of our prisoners kept in that castle, if either your prince or your beggar can gain the wisdom and grace to quiet his mind and hold himself contented with his situation and not desire to be somewhere else, that one is free to be just where he wills. He is not in prison. On the other hand, if either of them is let out of the castle prison, but still wishes to be somewhere other than where circumstances had placed him, he would lack the quality of freedom and would still be in prison.

VINCENT: Well, uncle, all these men whom you say are effectively in prison still view actual imprisonment as a very grave evil, while no man considers the kind of freedom that you are calling imprisonment to be an evil. They take no hurt from it and do not find it difficult. So while I cannot confute your logic, still—to speak plainly—my mind is not satisfied with these answers. They seem to be the kind of arguments that conclude but do not convince. The idea that every man is really in prison seems to me a sophistical fancy rather than a real circumstance.

ANTHONY: Bless your heart, cousin Vincent! In good faith I am happier with these words of yours than any you have so far spoken! If you had assented in words to what I said while your mind had departed unpersuaded, you would have lost the good fruit of it even if what I said was true. And on the other hand, if what I said was not true and I was deceived in thinking so, then in agreeing with me you would only have confirmed me in my folly. The truth is, cousin, that I am such an old fool and have looked at things in this way for so long that I can hardly think anything else to be true. But I would not want long habit to make me ashamed of changing my tune if the thing were not true. So let us consider the matter further, such that you can clearly understand me and I can more clearly understand myself. Spit on your hands boldly, and get a good grip, and do not accept anything against your own judgment, for that will bring us both closest to the truth!

VINCENT: Nay, uncle, I do not intend to take that line and to dispute with you. I haven't done it since we began; I have only wanted you to repeat some of your arguments for the further satisfaction of my own mind.

ANTHONY: Well, hold boldly to that resolution, cousin. For my part, I will entirely give up the point unless I can convince you— plainly convince you with no sophistry—that every man everywhere is a prisoner in a true prison, and also that there is no prince or king on the face of the earth who is not even more a prisoner, under this general kind of imprisonment, than many simple ignorant wretches who lie in an actual jail cell.

VINCENT: I would very much like to see these points proved, uncle.

ATNHONY: Then let me put a case to you: If a man were convicted of treason or some grave felony and condemned to death, but the specific time of his death was delayed until the king's pleasure in the matter was fully known, and he was put into the hands of keepers who held him in a place from which he could not escape—would that fellow, do you think, be a prisoner, or not?

VINCENT: What a question! If ever a man were a prisoner, it is that fellow in very deed.

ANTHONY: But now let us say that during the time between his condemnation and his execution he was given freedom to do what he wished—to have access to his lands and his wealth, and to have his wife and children and his friends and his servants about him. And let's add the detail that the place where he is kept is a royal castle with a great park and other comfortable pleasures surrounding it. And add if you like that he is even able to ride out when and where he wants, only with this one condition: that he is always under the eye of his keepers and he is unable to get away. He knows that whatever he does there is no way of escape, and that as soon as he is summoned he will go to his death. Now, cousin Vincent, what would you call this man? Is he a prisoner, since he is held for a sure execution? Or is he no prisoner at all, since in the meantime he is in such favorable circumstances and is allowed to do whatever he wants, except escape? Think carefully now, and do not give a quick answer that you will need to retract when you have had leisure to consider the matter.

VINCENT: No, uncle, I do not need to carefully consider the matter. It seems plain to me that despite all the favor he is shown and all the liberty he is granted, as long as that man is condemned to death and is being kept under a careful watch from which he cannot escape, he is still surely a prisoner.

ANTHONY: Well, cousin, I agree with you. But let me ask a further question. If there was another man who was thrown into jail for brawling, and was fettered in stocks and kept in a deep cell where he was left to stew for a time, but who knew that he was in no danger of death and that he would come out of the matter well enough—which of these two prisoners would be in the worse position? The one treated favorably, or the one more roughly handled?

VINCENT: By our Lady, uncle, I believe that most men would choose to lie in stocks for a time and then go free, rather than to walk about at liberty in a park only to be delivered to death.

ANTHONY: Well now, cousin, consider whether what I am about to say is mere sophistry or the very truth. I will tell you what I really think is true, but if you think otherwise, I will be glad to abandon the mistake that has beguiled me. It seems to me then that every man who is born into the world has been created by God, and comes into the world by God's providence. Is this sophistry?

VINCENT: Not at all uncle; it is a sure truth.

ANTHONY: This also I take for truth: that before any man or any woman emerges from the womb, they have been condemned to death through the original sin that they bring with them, contracted from the corrupted stock of our forefather Adam. Is this also true, cousin?

VINCENT: Very true indeed, uncle.

ANTHONY: Then further: it seems that God has placed all people on earth so securely that there is not a man, woman or child, no matter how much they might wander about and try, who can possibly find a way to escape from death. True, or imagined fancy, cousin?

VINCENT: This is no fancy, uncle. It is so clearly true that no one would be so silly as to deny it.

ANTHONY: Then I need say no more. You yourself grant that every person, even the greatest king on earth, is put here by the will of God in a particular place from which no man can escape. And you also grant that every person is under sure and safe keeping, waiting to be called forth by God, at which time he will certainly die. So, cousin, do you not grant that everyone in such a case is a prisoner?

VINCENT: I cannot help but see, uncle, that this must be so.

ANTHONY: And this would be true even if we were taken gently by the arm and led out of this world in a pleasant manner to our place of judgment. But the truth is that the greatest king on earth, no matter how freely he walks about or how powerful may be the armies among whom he rides, cannot escape this prison. He knows, unless he is a fool, that a sentence has already been delivered against him and that he will die. He may hope that the execution will be postponed for a time, but he can never be without fear—unless he manages to put the matter out of his mind—that either today or tomorrow that grisly hangman, Death, who has been lying in wait for him since he came into the world, will appear. And when Death does appear, he will not kneel before the man with reverence or pay attention to his royalty and his strength. No, he will fiercely grip him by the chest and make his bones rattle, and after many difficult torments he will strike him stark dead in his prison. He will then cast his body to the ground in a foul pit in some corner of the same prison, there to rot and be eaten by the wretched worms of the earth, and his soul will be sent to a yet more fearful judgment. And what might happen at that judgment is uncertain; the man will be in fear of eternal fire, even if by God's grace he is not without hope.

So you may plainly see that the whole earth is a prison, and that all men without exception, even those most at liberty within it who forget their true state and think themselves great lords, are no better than those who are cast into that narrow place we call a prison. All of them are already condemned to death. Now, cousin, I would be glad to know if you think all this a sophistical fancy, for I must tell you that I am unwise enough to think it a very plain truth indeed.

VINCENT: In good faith, I cannot resist your argument, uncle. You have proved your point that every man is a prisoner waiting for execution. And yet the hard treatment of actual imprisonment—the binding, bolting, stocking, lying on cold straw and other such trials—must make imprisonment much more odious and dreadful. For in that broad prison you speak of there is no such brutal handling of the prisoners.

ANTHONY: I think I said, cousin, that I hoped to prove to you that in this general prison—I mean the large prison of the whole world— people are dealt with in such a hard manner, and are so wrenched and wrung and painfully broken, that they have as much reason to grudge their state and as much horror at their condition as that wretch in the actual prison cell. If I could not prove it, I said that I would concede the point and change my mind. But the thing seems so plainly true to me that I doubt I will need to do that.

First grant me this point: that the prince and king of this broad prison of the world, as well as its chief jailor (though he has angels and devils who are sub-jailors under him) is God himself.

VINCENT: I will not deny that, uncle.

ANTHONY: If a man among us is committed to a prison and the prison-keeper is a good and honest fellow, the keeper will not maliciously torture the man or force his friends to pay extra to gain him a bit of ease. But if the prisoner becomes unruly and fights with his fellow prisoners or gets into some other kind of trouble, the keeper will treat him more harshly to keep his prison orderly. God, the keeper of the broad prison of this world, is neither cruel nor covetous. He has built the prison so securely that though it has no walls and lies open at every side, we can never find a way out of it no matter how far we go. He has no need to collar us and keep us in stocks for fear of our escaping. So he lets us walk around inside the prison and do what we will, as long as we live according to what he has shown us through reason and revelation.

Because of this temporary grace, we grow rebellious and we forget where we are. We do not remember that we are poor wretches in prison, and we begin to take ourselves for great lords. We portion out various parts of our prison through agreements and treaties, sometimes even through fraud and violence. We change the name of our prison and we call it our own land and livelihood. We garnish our prison with gold and make it glorious. In this prison men buy and sell; in this prison they fight and argue. They gamble and play at cards; they dance and revel. And in this prison many who are reputed to be honest and virtuous play the knave in private for their own pleasure.

We think ourselves at liberty because God allows all this. We abhor the state of those we call prisoners, thinking ourselves no prisoners at all. Under the false notion of our wealth and our freedom we foolishly forget both ourselves and our jail, along with the under-jail-ors—angels and devils both—and we forget even God himself. But though we forget God, God does not forget us; he sees us the whole time. And in his discontent at the way his rule is ignored in the jail, he sends the hangman—Death—to put many to execution, sometimes even by the thousands. Others undergo such severe sufferings that they are no better off than those who are placed in the actual prisons that you hold in such horror.

VINCENT: Most of what you say I will readily accept, uncle. But I must deny the idea that God, our chief jailor in this world, punishes people as if they were in prison, for I have never see him put a man in stocks or place chains on a man's legs; not even so much as lock a man in a room.

ANTHONY: Not every minstrel plays the harp, cousin, nor every singer the lute. A man may be a minstrel and make a melody with some other instrument; maybe a strangely fashioned one that has never been seen before. God, our head jailor, is invisible, so he uses visible instruments in his punishments. They do not look like the instruments a jailor uses, but they have a similar effect. He brings a hot fever that will make a man as uncomfortable as if he were lying on the cold ground. He wrings a man's head with a migraine, bolts his neck with a sore throat, and binds his arms with paralysis. He manacles his hands with gout and ties his legs with cramp. He binds a man to his bed with a sore back, and there the fellow lies, as unable to rise as if he were held fast with his feet in the stocks.

If there were folk who had been born and raised in a prison, and who had never looked out the door or over the wall and had never heard of another world outside, and if they called "prisoners" those among them who were locked up in a narrow room for doing bad deeds, they would think themselves as free and at large as we do now. And we are as deceived as they are when we think ourselves to be something other than prisoners.

VINCENT: I cannot deny all that you have said, uncle. But for all that, it is still the case that if we are ever taken prisoner by the Turk, we will be in a much narrower prison than we now are, with less freedom of movement. And there might be much worse to follow. So there is little surprise that men want to avoid it.

ANTHONY: That is well said, cousin. I am only speaking about our consolation in the midst of this time, and I say that we can take comfort in the fact that our imagination deceives us into thinking that imprisonment will be worse than it is, because we now think ourselves more free than we really are. As for the sufferings that accompany imprisonment, they seem to me so slight that we should be ashamed to think about them in such a great cause as suffering for Christ. Many good men and women willingly suffer the loss of their liberty without being forced to do so, such as the holy monks of the Charterhouse, who never leave their cells except to go to Church, and the women of the order of St. Bridget, and of St. Clare, and all manner of enclosed religious orders. Yet they are happy during many long years, often even happier than those who walk about freely in the world. So you see that the loss of liberty is a horror enhanced by our own fancy.

I once knew a charitable woman who regularly visited a poor prisoner in jail. He had made the place warm enough, with mats of straw underfoot and around the walls, and she was glad for his general health. But among the many sufferings that she lamented for his sake, one in particular troubled her: that every night the door was locked by the jailor and the man was shut up inside the cell from outside. "By my troth," she said, "if my door were shut upon me like that, I think I would be unable to breathe!" At that the prisoner laughed inwardly. He dared not laugh out loud, for he stood in awe of her, and was dependent on her charitable alms for much of his food; but he laughed in his mind because he knew that every night she shut her chamber door and locked it tight, along with all her windows, and would not open them again until morning. What difference could it make, he thought, whether the door was locked from the inside or the outside?

As to other sufferings that often accompany imprisonment, I am not so silly as to say that they are not grievous; but I do say that our fear often imagines them to be greater than they are. And as great as they are, many have endured them, men and women both, and have come through them well enough.

But I would further ask: what have we determined in our hearts to do? Are we ready to suffer a measure of bodily pain for the one who suffered such great pains for us, or do we plan to run from him and utterly forsake him rather than suffer any pain at all? Those in this last category—may God keep us all from it!—are in no need of comfort since they run away from suffering, and I am afraid they will have little use for good advice if God's grace has fled so far from them. But if we have determined to stay faithful to our Savior no matter what suffering may come, then I can see no need for shrinking from the sufferings of imprisonment. Whatever may happen to us—whether our imprisonment is long or short, its pains light or heavy—all is in the hands of the one for whose sake we are enduring the suffering, and who will not let anyone be tested beyond what each can bear.

And speaking of the horror of imprisonment, how foolish we would be if we feared the kind of imprisonment the Turk might impose on us, and not fear the much worse prison that will be our fate if we forsake Christ—I mean the prison of hell. The Turk's imprisonment is always temporary; but no one in hell shall ever get out of it. How foolish it would be to avoid the easier prison only to fall into the worse one! How sad to exchange a short imprisonment that would have won us everlasting freedom, for a prison that will never let us go.

Joseph was in prison while his brothers were free and at large; yet later they came to him looking for their food. Daniel was in prison with wild beasts around him, yet God protected him and brought him out safely. Let us not doubt that God will do the same for us, or perhaps treat us even better by letting us die there. John the Baptist was in prison all the time that Herod and Herodias were feasting and making merry and Salome was delighting them with her dancing, until she danced his very head off. And now? St. John sits at God's table in the great high feast of heaven, while Herod and Herodias sit burning in hell, and the devil mocks them by dancing with their daughter in the fire.

To culminate all, let us remember that our Savior himself was taken prisoner for our sake. As a prisoner he was hauled from the garden; as a prisoner he was kept in chains; as a prisoner he was brought before Annas the High Priest; from there as a prisoner he was carried to Caiaphas. Then as a prisoner he was taken to Pilate, and as a prisoner sent to King Herod and brought back again. To the end of his passion he was imprisoned. It is true that the time of his imprisonment was not long; but in that short time he endured more than most prisoners face in a much longer time. When we think of all this, and when we remember his innocence and his willingness to suffer imprisonment for our sakes, we must be ungrateful cowards if we would abandon him for fear of our own imprisonment.

XVIII.

On the fear of a shameful and painful death.

VINCENT: Dear uncle, if I can remember all these things I am now hearing from you about imprisonment (and our Lord reward you for them!) I think that with the help of God's grace I will not fear it, nor ever forsake the faith of our Savior because of it. But we now come to the very center of the dread that makes this incursion of the noonday devil—the open invasion of the Turk and his persecution against the faith—seem so terrible to us. It may be that by God's help we can vanquish all these other troubles, the loss of our goods, our lands, and our liberty. But when we remember the terror of shameful and painful death, all that was meant to comfort us falls into oblivion. In the face of that threat, I fear that most of us find our fervor ebbing away and our hearts becoming so faint that we are near to falling from very fear.

ANTHONY: I agree, cousin, that this is indeed the sorest pinch. Yet here too you can see that our dread increases or diminishes according to the way our affections have been fashioned beforehand and been rooted in our minds. This is so true that you may find a person who so loves his wealth that he fears the loss of his lands more than the loss of his life. You may even see someone endure deadly tortures of the kind that another would prefer to die rather than encounter, all to avoid telling where he has hidden his money. I do not doubt that you have heard many true stories of people who for various reasons have willingly suffered painful and tormenting deaths. It is all a question of the quality of a person's loves.

The mind becomes imprinted with affections and loves in different ways. One way is through our bodily senses that find things physically pleasant or unpleasant. This kind of affection is common to men and animals. Another way of imprinting affections is through the use of reason, which orders the affections of the senses and also disposes the mind to spiritual virtues that are often opposed to the clamor of the senses. These loves that come through reason belong to men and not to beasts. The devil, our spiritual enemy, tries to inflame our bestial affections, while almighty God, our true friend, moves us by his Holy Spirit toward spiritual loves. He instructs our reason to pursue such loves by receiving them as they are sown in our souls, and by watering them with good counsel and continual prayer so that they take deep root. According to the affections of our hearts will be our strength or our weakness in the face of the terror of death. So, cousin, let us consider what our reason has to say toward mastering the fear that comes from sensual affections. And though we may not entirely avoid such fear, let us at least try to bridle it so that it cannot act like a headstrong horse and carry us away to the devil against our wills.

XIX.

On death considered only as the end of this life.

THE first thing to do is to consider and carefully weigh this thing that we so mightily dread: namely painful and shameful death. And I notice that when you consistently join to "death" the qualities of "painful" and "shameful," you imply that death would be much less fearsome if it came along without either shame or pain.

VINCENT: Yes, uncle, without a doubt it would be much less fearsome. Though for all that, I know many men who are very reluctant to die even were it to come without either.

ANTHONY: I well believe it, cousin, and more's the pity. The reason for fear of death is almost always either a lack of faith, a lack of hope, or a lack of intelligence. Those who do not believe in a life to come and who think themselves wealthy here on earth are of course very unhappy to leave this life, since they think they would lose everything. This is the origin of that foolish and unfaithful saying so common among us: "This world we know, and the other world we do not know." Some will even say in sport—though I think they are being serious—that "the devil is not as black as he is painted," and "let him be as black as he wants, he is still no blacker than a crow!" and many other such foolish fancies.

There are others who really do believe in a life to come, but because of their lewd lives they have lost the hope of salvation. I am hardly surprised that such people are reluctant to die. There may be some among them whose reluctance is founded on a firm purpose of repentance, and who are hoping that they might have a little time left on earth to amend their ways. And though the desire to die and be with God seems to me as good a means for purchasing remission of sin as many years of penance, this kind of reluctance to die may gain God's approval. There are also some who are reluctant to die, and yet at the same time who are very glad to die and who long to be dead.

VINCENT: That seems a strange attitude, uncle!

ANTHONY: I do not think it occurs often, but sometimes it does. St. Paul was one such. His longing for God led him to wish for death; but to profit others he was content to continue here in pain, and to defer his inestimable bliss in heaven. As he said, "My desire is to depart and be with Christ, for that is far better. But to remain in the flesh is more necessary on your account" (Phil. 1:23–24). In any case, considering death alone apart from any shame or pain that may accompany it, no one who has faith would hesitate to depart from this world with a very good will. They would know that their death, especially if suffered for faithfulness to Christ, would cleanse all their sins and send them straight to heaven. And even if shame and pain accompanied death, many among them would willingly suffer death, knowing that rejecting their faith to avoid death would sever them from God. Even for the gain of the whole world and the profit of everyone in it, it cannot be a loving thing to displease the One who made it.

Some others, as I said, do not want to die because of lack of intelligence. Though they believe in the world to come and hope to arrive there, they are so taken with the love of the things of this world that they want to keep hold of them as long as they can, and they fight tooth and nail not to give them up. When finally they can no longer enjoy this world, and death forces its way upon them, they reluctantly agree to be taken to heaven and to God, since nothing better can be arranged! Such people are being very foolish, like that silly man who when he was a child had filled his play-purse with cherry pits, and he took such a liking to his false treasure that when he grew up he would not exchange it for a larger purse filled with gold. They are like the snail in Aesop's fable. You remember that Jupiter (whom the poets used as a figure of the mighty God) invited all the worms of the world to a great feast. But the snail would not come, and instead stayed at home. When Jupiter later asked her why she did not come to enjoy the feast he had prepared where she would be warmly welcomed and would enjoy the many delights and pleasures of his great palace, she told him that nothing pleased her so much as being in her own house. Jupiter grew very angry at this, and said that since she loved her home so well, she would never go anywhere without carrying it on her back. By that fable Aesop was touching on the folly of people who set their hearts on a small pleasure and are then unable to put it aside for gaining something far better, often to their own great harm.

I am afraid that there are many such Christian folk who carry their goods on their backs like that snail, and who are so reluctant to leave their little house that they cannot find it in their hearts to go with a good will to the great feast God has prepared for them in heaven. Unless they mend their ways, I fear that they will fare much worse than Aesop's snail. They are only too likely to have their little house bound on their backs forever. Not only will they be unable to creep slowly about like the snail under her burden, but they will lie bound under their feeble possessions with the fire of hell raging around them. They are like a drunken man, who will not be forgiven for the evil he does in his drunkenness, because he placed himself in that condition by his own willful folly.

VINCENT: I am afraid you are right, uncle, that there are many people who fall into that kind of folly through their own fault. Yet if this is to be a fool, then there are many such fools who think themselves very wise.

ANTHONY: Fools who think themselves wise? By our Lady, cousin, I have never yet met a fool who did not think himself wise! Just as it shows a spark of sobriety in a drunken head when he realizes he is drunk and hauls himself to bed, so it is a little spark of intelligence, and a rare one, when a fool perceives himself to be foolish.

VINCENT: I think, uncle, that you have addressed this fear of death well. For if by losing this life we will find a better one, reason tells us that it would be foolish to forsake the faith for loss of life. There remains only this one matter: the shame and pain accompanying death. May I ask you to give us some comfort in the face of those two horrors?

XX.

*Concerning the shame that accompanies death
in being persecuted for the faith.*

ANTHONY: I think that even in the face of those grievous qualities—shame, I mean, and also pain—a man who reasons well will
not be so abashed by them as to forsake his faith. Let us begin with
shame. How can any wise and faith-filled man be filled with dread
at the shame of death, when both his reason and his faith clearly tell
him that there is no shame at all in such a death? Is it possible that to
die for the faith, to die united to Christ in faith, hope and charity, is
anything but glorious? "Precious in the eyes of the Lord is the death
of his saints," says the Scripture (Ps. 116:15). If the death of the saints
is glorious and valiant in the eyes of God, it can never be shameful,
whatever it may seem to be in the sight of men. It was not only at
the death of St. Stephen that God and heaven opened up around
him. When any man dies for the faith, God and the whole of heaven's
company are looking on and witnessing his passion.

Imagine, cousin, that you were being led along a broad main
street of a great city, and all along the way, on one side of the street, a
rabble of ragged beggars and madmen were hurling all the shameful
names and villainous accusations at you that they could think of. And
all along the other side of the street was ranged a large company of
wise and good people, fifteen times the number of the rabble on the

opposite side, praising you and commending your behavior. Would you turn back because of the shameful jesting and railing of those foolish wretches? Or would you rather keep on with good cheer and a glad heart, encouraged and honored by the praise of that good and honorable company?

VINCENT: No doubt of it, uncle: I would pay attention to the high regard of the commendable people, and not pay a moment's notice to the railing of all those ribalds.

ANTHONY: So it is with the man of faith. He can never account himself shamed on earth by any kind of death he suffers for the sake of Christ. However vile and shameful it may seem in the sight of a few worldly wretches, it is praised and commended as precious and honorable in the sight of God and the glorious company of heaven, who are as present and as watchful of his death as all those foolish people. Heaven's company outnumbers them by more than a hundred to one, and each one of that heavenly band is a hundred times more worthy to be regarded than a hundred whole rabbles of the other.

A man who was so mad as to be ashamed to confess the name of Christ because he feared such a rebuke would be fleeing from a mere shadow of shame only to fall into true shame—and a deadly painful shame it would be indeed! Our Savior made a promise that he himself would be ashamed of such a man before his Father in heaven and in the presence of all his holy angels, as you may read in the ninth chapter of Luke's gospel. What manner of shameful shame will that be? If a man's cheeks sometimes redden with shame in this world, how will they burn with fire for shame when Christ shows himself ashamed of them in heaven!

The blessed apostles considered it a great glory to suffer for Christ, the very thing we foolish people think to be villainy and shame. When they were scourged by the Jewish authorities and commanded to stop speaking the name of Christ, "they left the presence of the council, rejoicing that they were counted worthy to suffer dishonor for the name" (Acts 5:41). They were so proud of the shame and the pain they had received that they continued to preach about Jesus despite the council's orders, not only in the Temple where they had earlier been taken and whipped, but doubling their activity from house to house.

We are so concerned about being esteemed by worldly people despite all the wicked things they do, that I wish we would emulate them in some of the good things they practice. It is a custom among them that they send their children to suitable masters who can teach them a trade or a handicraft, and so help them make their way in the world. When such a youth disdains to obey his master, and refuses to do the very things that the master himself did when he was a servant learning the trade, the young fellow is thought to be nothing but a proud ingrate who would never be likely to succeed. Let us consider and weigh well this practice: Our master Christ, who is not only the master but the maker of the whole world, was willing for our sakes to undergo the most villainous and shameful death that the world then knew. He endured mocking and contempt joined with horrible pain, as when he was crowned with thorns and the blood ran down his face. He was given a reed as a scepter, and they knelt before him and scornfully saluted him like a king, and beat upon the sharp thorns around his head. Our Savior told us that a disciple is not above his master. Since our master endured so much painful shame, we must be proud creatures indeed if we disdain to follow in our master's steps. He ascended through shame to glory; but for fear of a temporary worldly shame we would prefer to fall into everlasting shame in the eyes of heaven and hell, rather than to join him in everlasting glory.

XXI.

Concerning the pain that accompanies death
through persecution.

VINCENT: I think you need not take any more pains to discuss this matter of shame, uncle. Any man with reason in his head should hold himself satisfied with what you have explained. But to tell the truth, the real pinch is in the pain. I can see well enough that a wise man might master his fear of shame such that it would hardly move him at all; it has even become a common proverb among us that "shame is as it is taken." But, by God, uncle, all the wisdom and wit in the world can never master pain so as to keep it from being painful!

ANTHONY: It is certainly true, cousin, that no person can use his reason to change the nature of pain such that he no longer feels it. Unless pain is felt, it is not pain at all. The only man who can allow his leg to be stricken off at the knee without grief is the one whose head was struck off half an hour earlier! Yet reason can still help a reasonable man to accept pain when it would be harmful not to do so. While he would not foolishly welcome pain without any cause, he would be glad enough to sustain it when there was good reason, whether to gain a great profit or avoid a great loss, or perhaps to avoid suffering a far worse pain.

We see this in many less important cases than that of suffering for the faith. It is painful to take bitter medicines, and to have our flesh lanced and cut. A child or a childish person is unwilling to abide that kind of pain and so avoids it, allowing his sickness or sore to grow until it becomes incurable. But a wiser person, who would be as eager as the faint-hearted to avoid suffering if there was no good reason for it, nonetheless takes his medicine and submits to the surgeon's knife, since his reason tells him that he will gain by his suffering. If reason alone is enough to move us to endure pain in order to gain some worldly pleasure or to avoid a yet worse pain, why should reason not be even more powerful when united to faith and grace to help us in our current difficulties? Why should it not engender in us a desire, and through long and deep meditation bring us to a deep-rooted habitual readiness, to patiently suffer painful death so that we can gain the rich and everlasting life of heaven and avoid the everlasting pains of hell?

VINCENT: In truth, uncle, if faith is presupposed, as you have insisted from the beginning of our conversation, I cannot find any words to reasonably counter your arguments. Yet I remember that fable by Aesop about the old stag who was being chased by a little hunting dog. You remember how it went. The stag had outpaced the dog, and as he rested on the way he talked the situation over with a fellow deer. They reasoned together that if the stag continued running, the dog might come upon him when he was exhausted and unable to fight, whereas if he turned and fought the dog now, he could defeat him with his superior strength and the use of his antlers before the hunters could come up and give help. So the two deer determined to stay and fight. But when the dog picked up the scent and came baying and yelping at them, they entirely forgot their resolution and turned tail and ran!

I am afraid the same sort of thing would easily happen to me and to many others. We might reason together and agree to act as you say—and really think we would do it—but as soon as those hellhounds the Turks came yelping and howling upon us, our hearts would run away from us as quickly as those other harts fled from the hounds.

ANTHONY: I suppose, cousin, that without the help of grace our reasoning will leave us pretty much in the same condition as those brute beasts. But God not only gives us our reason; he also imparts the power to rule ourselves by it. Unless we willingly cast aside our reasoning and the grace that accompanies it, God is always ready to maintain it within us and even to increase it. As the Lord bids us through the Psalmist, "do not be like a horse or a mule (or a stag!) that has no understanding" (Ps. 32:9). So cousin, let us be confident that if we apply our minds to gathering courage and comfort against our persecution, and if we listen to the voice of reason and let it sink into our hearts—not vomiting it up or choking and stifling it by stuffing our stomachs with worldly vanities—God will work in us and will provide all the strength that we need. Then our hearts will not be shameful and cowardly and we will not forsake our Savior and so lose our salvation, no matter how bitter or sharp the pain—always a temporary one—might be.

VINCENT: All very well, uncle; but every man naturally fears pain and is very reluctant to meet it.

ANTHONY: Yes, and no one suggests that anyone should go running toward it unless he is captured and cannot flee. Yet if that should happen, reason then tells us that we should endure the shorter pain here so that we can avoid a much greater and longer pain in hell.

VINCENT: I recently heard of a man who responded to a similar line of thinking with the following argument, uncle. He said that if a person were to stand firm from the first in his confession of faith and was thereby brought to torture, it could happen that he would forsake his Savior in the bitterness of the pain, and so die in his sin and be damned forever. Whereas if he went a different route and forsook his faith at the beginning and just for a time—doing it only in word and keeping faith in his heart—he might save himself from the danger of that painful death and afterwards ask God's mercy. He might then live a long life and do many good deeds, and be saved the same way that St. Peter was.

ANTHONY: That man's reason, cousin, is like a three-footed stool, so unstable and tottering on every side that whoever sits on it will soon take a nasty spill. Here are the three legs of that unsafe stool: false fear, false faith, and false flattering hope.

First, this fear, that by confessing Christ at the beginning the man might later be overcome by pain and thereby be damned, is false and fantastic. As if God would not be readier to forgive a man like this than he would to forgive the one who put no confidence in him and would not endure any pain at all for his sake! As if the more a man suffered for God, the worse God would treat him! If this were so, our Savior would never have said "Do not fear those who can kill the body, and after that do no more" (Luke 12:4). He would instead have said, "Fear and hold in dread those who can kill the body, for by means of inflicting a painful death they may make you forsake me and you will be damned forever!"

The second leg of the tottering stool is false faith. It is nothing but a pretend-faith when a man says to God that he secretly believes in him, trusts him, and loves him, and then openly dishonors him and flatters his enemies by forsaking him before the eyes of the world. Either the man has no faith at all and does not perceive that our Lord is present everywhere and looks angrily at his betrayal, or he is in open rebellion and dishonors God to his very face.

The third leg of this unstable stool is a false flattering hope. We know that to forsake the faith because of fear is forbidden by God upon the pain of eternal death. And though it is true that God in his goodness forgives many who have fallen, to presume upon that forgiveness is a false and pestilential hope, and will lead a man straight to his own destruction.

Those who fall because of fear or some other passion and then attempt to rise again, consoling themselves with the hope of God's grace and forgiveness, are walking a secure road to salvation. But what of a man who encourages himself to sin with the idea that God's mercy will follow later? I have no power to keep God from pardoning whomever he will, and I pray that such a person will gain a pardon. But I am very much afraid that he would not receive what he looks for. I cannot remember any example or any promise in Scripture where an offender like this was offered grace after his offense. It seems instead that this type of presumption, going under the guise of hope, draws near to the abominable sin of blasphemy against the Holy Spirit. And we are told in the gospels of St. Matthew and St. Mark that there is no possibility of gaining forgiveness for that sin, or at least great difficulty, whether in this world or in the world to come.

You say that the man looked to the example of St. Peter, who abandoned our Savior and was granted forgiveness afterward. But let that man reconsider the matter, and see that St. Peter did not forsake Christ by following a plan of sinful trust; he was overcome and vanquished by a sudden fear. And Peter did not thereby avoid trouble, but only delayed it for a short time. For he quickly repented of his deed and wept bitterly over it. And then on the day of Pentecost he again confessed loyalty to his master, and was soon imprisoned for it, and was later scourged and again put in prison. And once delivered from prison, he did not stop his preaching until after long labors and troubles he suffered cruel torments and was slain in Rome. In the same way I suspect that anyone who denies our Savior and afterward gains forgiveness will pay for it in some way or other before he comes to heaven.

VINCENT: Yet such a person may perhaps gain forgiveness through penances during life, and thereby die a natural death and escape a violent one. For violent death is always painful.

ANTHONY: It may be that he will not avoid a violent death in any case, for God can bring him to death in many different ways. But you seem to think that whoever dies a natural death does so like a pleasure-seeker at his ease. You remind me of a man who once went to sea in a small boat. He had never been to sea before, and as the waves grew rough he was tossed hither and thither. The poor man groaned in spirit and thought he was going to die. He said to himself, "Would to God that I were on land, so that I might die in peace!" He thought that the waves and all their tossing were keeping him from dying, and that if he could only gain the land he would die there in comfort.

VINCENT: Yes, uncle, death is painful to every man. But a natural death is not nearly as painful as a violent one.

ANTHONY: It seems to me, cousin, that any death that fetches a man against his will by force, even if some call it "natural," is violent. And that kind of violent death occurs whenever a man is sorry to die and would live longer if only he could. But I would be interested to know who told you that there is little or no pain in a "natural" death? From what I can see, people who die naturally are usually afflicted with a disease. If the pain of the days or weeks in which they lay pining in their beds were gathered into a time as short as the man who suffers a violent death, I suspect that it would make double the amount of pain. Such a person suffers more, not less. And some are in great pain for many days, nearly as great as the pain that rids a man of his life in less than half an hour. I think many of them would be happy to go by way of a shorter and sharper pang. Or do you suppose that it hurts more to have a knife cut the flesh from the outside than if the knife began on the inside and cut its way outward? I have heard some on their deathbed complain that they felt as though sharp knives were cutting their heartstrings in two. Some feel as though their brains were being pricked full of pins. Some who suffer pleurisy say that they feel a sharp sword stab them in the heart every time they cough.

XXII.

On the pains of hell.

BUT what need have we to compare natural to violent death in this matter? The one who forsakes Christ for fear of a violent death is in danger of finding his natural death a thousand times more painful. For his natural death has everlasting pain knit so instantly to it that there is not a moment of time between the end of the one and the beginning of the other, and that other will have no end. It was not without good reason that Christ gave us so solemn a warning. "I tell you, my friends, do not fear those who kill the body, and after that have no more that they can do. But I will warn you whom to fear: fear him who, after he has killed, has power to cast into hell; yes, I tell you, fear him!" (Luke 12:4–5). By this warning Christ was not saying that we should never fear those who can do us bodily harm. He meant that we should not fear them so much that for dread of them we would displease the one who can everlastingly kill both body and soul with a never-dying death.

Dear God, cousin, if a man would weigh well these words of Christ, and let them sink deeply into his heart, it would be enough to enable him to treat all the Great Turk's threats as nothing, and to esteem him less than a straw. We should be happy to endure all the pain that the world could bring upon us, rather than to cast ourselves into the pain of hell, a pain a hundred thousand times more intolerable, and one that will never end. What a woeful death that is, in which they are forever dying and yet can never once be dead! As Scripture says, "They long for death, but it comes not, and dig for it more than for hidden treasures, and they rejoice and are glad when they find the grave (Job 3:21–22). If a man could choose between them, who would not suffer the most terrible death that all the Turks in Turkey could devise for a whole year, rather than endure for even half an hour that undying death? What a wretched folly for folk of feeble faith to fall into such a terrible torment only to avoid a much shorter and less grievous pain!

So I think, cousin, that if we have genuine faith and if we use our reason, if we believe and think often and well on the matter, the fear of the Turk's persecution—all that the noonday devil may do to try to force us to forsake the faith—will never be able to turn us from Christ.

VINCENT: I do believe you are right, uncle. If we would think more often of the pains of hell, a thing that many are very reluctant to do and purposely try to distract themselves from, this one point would produce many martyrs.

XXIII.

On the joys of heaven.

ANTHONY: To speak truth, cousin, if we were the kind of Christians we should be, I would not for very shame want to speak of the pains of hell as a motivation for keeping Christ's faith. I would much rather remind us of the joys of heaven and of the goodness to be gained there. But God is wonderfully merciful in this matter. By speaking to us of hell and teaching us to fear it, many men and women now sit or will sit gloriously crowned in heaven who would never have set a foot toward it had they not been afraid of hell.

We cannot sufficiently conceive either the joys of heaven or the pains of hell. But if we could, we would be much more moved to suffer for Christ to win heaven's joys than to avoid hellish pains. We fleshly folk are so drowned in our desire for carnal pleasure that we naturally dread their loss more than we desire spiritual pleasure in the joyful hope of heaven. But if we could withdraw our hearts from our physical appetites through prayer and God's grace, we would draw nearer to the secret inward pleasure of the Spirit, and gain a foretaste of the incomparable and inconceivable joy that will be ours, God willing, in heaven. It is written, "I shall be satisfied in beholding your face in glory" (Ps. 17:15). The desire and heavenly hope of that vision will be a greater encouragement to suffer for the love of God than any dread of the pain endured by the damned in hell.

In the meantime, if we have not experienced the foretaste of heaven that God sometimes gives his special servants, let us try to cultivate through prayer such a fervent longing for heaven's joys in our hearts that in order to attain them we will count as nothing all fleshly delights, all worldly pleasures, all earthly losses, and all bodily torments and pains. We are not told explicitly what heaven's joys will be, but God has told us that they will be great. "The souls of the righteous will shine forth like the sun, and will run like sparks through the stubble" (Wis. 3:7).

If you tell a carnally minded man about this kind of pleasure, he will take little pleasure in it. If you say that in heaven his body will be unchanging and beyond all harm, he will only fear that he will lose the pleasure of eating and drinking. If you tell him that he will never need sleep, he will complain about losing the pleasure he gains from lying slug-abed. If you tell him that we will live like the angels and not be involved in the act of generation, he will only feel the loss of his filthy voluptuous vices. He will then tell you that he is fine just as he is, and that he does not want to give up this world for the next. As St. Paul says, "the unspiritual man does not receive the gifts of the Spirit of God, for they are folly to him, and he is not able to understand them because they are spiritually discerned" (1 Cor. 2:14). Yet the time will come when all these foul pleasures will be taken from him, and it will be painful for him even to think of them. We have a shadow of that experience when we are in the grip of a serious illness and cannot stand to look at any food or even to think of lust. When that happens, and a person gains even a glimmering of the heavenly joys that he had counted so cheap, O good God, how glad he would then be to give up this whole world for even a little part in those joys!

Though we cannot now fully experience the delight in thinking about heaven's spiritual joys that we should, let us fill our eyes with reading, our ears with hearing, our mouths with reciting, and our hearts with meditating on the joyful words of holy Scripture that speak of their wonder and greatness. As it is, our carnal hearts and our dull worldly wits can hardly conceive even a shadow of their true substance. I say a shadow, for no one living in this world can behold the glorious face of God. The best and most virtuous person living is as far from a true conception of it as a man born blind is from the proper imagination of colors. "No eye has seen, nor ear heard, nor the heart of man conceived, what God has prepared for those who love him" (1 Cor. 2:9). The joys of heaven are so far beyond the state of this world that they excel anything we can possibly imagine.

And beyond these joys, our Lord tells us by the mouth of St. John that those who suffer for his sake will receive a special reward. He says, "To him who conquers I will grant to eat of the tree of life." And he says further, "Do not fear anything you may suffer... but be faithful unto death, and I will give you the crown of life, and you shall not be harmed by the second death." And, "To him who conquers I will give some of the hidden manna, and I will give him a white stone, with a new name written on the stone which no one knows except him who receives it." And "He who conquers will wear white garments, and I will confess his name before my Father and before his angels." And, "He who conquers, I will make a pillar in the temple of my God; never shall he go out of it, and I will write on him the name of my God, and the name of the city of my God, the new Jerusalem which comes down from my God out of heaven, and my own new name" (Rev. 2:7; 10; 17; 3:5; 12). In these and other such passages we can see how far these heavenly joys surpass all the comfort that ever came into the mind of anyone living here upon earth.

The blessed apostle Paul often spoke of his many sufferings. He said that he had been "in far greater labors, far more imprisonments, with countless beatings, and often near death. Five times I have received at the hands of the Jews the forty lashes less one. Three times I have been beaten with rods; once I was stoned. Three times I have been shipwrecked; a night and a day I have been adrift at sea; on frequent journeys, in danger from rivers, danger from robbers, danger from my own people, danger from Gentiles, danger in the city, danger in the wilderness, danger at sea, danger from false brethren; in toil and hardship, through many a sleepless night, in hunger and thirst, often without food, in cold and exposure. And, apart from other things, there is the daily pressure upon me of my anxiety for all the churches" (2 Cor. 11:23–28). Yet despite all these troubles that continued for so many years, he spoke of his suffering as very light in comparison with what was coming. "For this slight momentary affliction is preparing for us an eternal weight of glory beyond all comparison, because we look not to the things that are seen but to the things that are unseen; for the things that are seen are transient, but the things that are unseen are eternal" (2 Cor. 4:17–18).

No member of the Christian body can come to this great glory apart from the head. Our head is Christ, and if we wish to gain heaven we must be joined to him and follow him as his members. He has gone before us, and he is the guide who will lead us there. Whoever wishes to enter that realm "must walk the same way that Christ walked" (1 John 2:6). What was the way along which Christ walked into heaven? He showed us when he spoke to the two disciples on the road to Emmaus. "Was it not necessary that the Christ should suffer these things and so enter into his glory?" (Luke 24:26). Who for very shame can desire to enter the Kingdom of Christ with ease, when he himself entered his kingdom with so much pain?

XXIV.

Concerning the painful death of Christ.

As I have said before, cousin, if we would only ponder the example of our Savior himself, that example alone should be enough to encourage all true Christians to bear the loss of worldly goods, to submit to captivity, slavery, and imprisonment, and to gladly endure worldly shame. And I will now say the same thing concerning painful death. Only consider Christ's bitter passion: the many bloody strokes his cruel tormentors gave him with rods and whips upon every part of his body; the scornful crown of thorns beaten down upon his head causing his blood to stream down from every side; his limbs drawn and stretched upon the cross, straining his veins and sinews and inflicting pains and cruel cramps at every moment; the long nails driven through his hands and his feet; his body lifted up and left to hang in horrible pain, with all its weight bearing down upon the wounded places pierced with nails. And all the while he experienced no pity from his tormentors, but only great contempt from them, as he suffered many hours until he gave his soul willingly to his Father. And afterwards, consider that his torturers were not content with their malice, but pierced his heart with a sharp spear from which blood and water flowed, the secret source of the inestimable strength of the sacraments. If we would only consider his incomparable kindness in all this, our cold hearts would become inflamed with the fire of his love, and we would not only be willing, but would be glad to suffer death for the one who endured such a death for our sakes.

Only think of the burning love many human lovers have shown for those upon whom they have set their affection. You know, not only from old written stories, but from lived experience in every country whether Christian or heathen, how such lovers have endured many labors, risked their lives and even lost them, being content that their lovers might see how faithful in love they were by their suffering and death. Does it not shame us in our cold affection toward God that we would consider forsaking our Savior out of fear of temporary death? Would not a lover, who was ready to die for his love even if he were to gain no reward from it, be exceedingly happy to die twice for her, if he knew that death would not mean separation from her, but instead would mean that he could dwell with her in pleasure and delight forever? What cold lovers we are to refuse and forsake Christ, when he has so arranged things that we will not only live with him in heaven, but also reign with him! As St. Paul says, "If we suffer with him, we shall reign with him" (2 Tim. 2:11).

How many noble hearts, Romans and others of many countries, willingly gave their lives and suffered deadly pains for their countries to win worldly fame and renown! And should we shrink to suffer as much for eternal honor and the everlasting glory of heaven? Even heretics in the devil's keeping are at times so obstinate that they readily endure a painful death for a vain glory. Is it not more than shameful that Christ sees his own Catholics forsake their faith rather than suffer death for true glory? Of this I am sure: that if we had a fifteenth part of the love for Christ that he has for us, all the pains of the Turk's persecution could not keep us from him, and there would be as many martyrs here in Hungary as in the days of old.

Imagine, cousin, that the Turk was here with his whole army, and was fiercely attacking us and devising all manner of torments for us if we did not renounce the faith. And to increase our terror his army came upon us screaming and shouting, with trumpets blaring and timbrels banging and all their guns exploding in a fearful noise. Then imagine that at the very same time the earth suddenly began to quake and was rent apart, and all the devils of hell rose up and showed themselves in their ugly and fearsome shapes, screeching with hideous howling, and all hell lay open to us so that we could look down into that pestilential pit and see the swarm of poor souls in their terrible torments. In such a case I doubt that we would even remember that the Turk's army was present at all.

And further: imagine that in the midst of all this we were given a sight of the great glory of God: the Trinity in his high marvelous majesty, our Savior sitting on his throne with his immaculate Mother and the whole company of heaven, and all of them calling us to join them. I am sure that we would run toward them as quickly as we could, even if all the Turk's tormenters and all the devils of hell lay between us.

Let us consider these things well, and count on the sure help of God. We will then lay hold of his promise, and the truth will surround us like a shield, and we will fear nothing. Let us prepare our minds beforehand for whatever may come, and place all our trust in God's help, not trusting at all in our own strength. Let us not desire to be brought to persecution—after all it is a proud mind that desires martyrdom—but let us pray to be ready to suffer it with the strength and help of God should it come to pass.

And meanwhile, let us be resolute in fasting, prayer, and giving alms, and let us be ready to give to God whatever might be taken from us. If the devil promises that we can keep our lands and our goods, let us remember that in any case we cannot keep them long. If he frightens us with exile, let us remember that we were not born to be stuck in one place like a tree, and that God will be with us wherever we go. If he threatens us with captivity, let us answer him that it is better to be a slave of men for a short time than to be the devil's prisoner in hell forever. If he puts into our minds the terror of the Turk, let us remember that the Turk is only a shadow, and all his evil a mere flea-bite compared to the devil's malice. For it is not the Turk who is behind all of this, but the devil himself, as our Lord has said, "The devil will cast some of you into prison to test you" (Rev. 2:10). Therefore St. Paul says, "Our warfare is not against flesh and blood" (Eph. 6:12).

The devil uses men to make us fear him; but unless we fall into fear, he cannot harm us. Therefore St. James says, "Resist the devil and he will flee from you" (James 4:7). The devil never attacks and seizes a man until he perceives that he is already down on the ground. He sends his human servants to tumble us into fear, and runs around us like a roaring and ramping lion, as St. Peter says: "Your adversary the devil goes about like a roaring lion, seeking someone to devour" (1 Pet. 5:8). He seeks those who have fallen so that he can devour them. It is not wise, then, to think so constantly about the Turks and to forget the devil. What a fool a man would be if he was worried about getting bitten by a little growling cur when a rampant lion was about to attack him. When the devil roars at us through the threats of mortal men, let us perceive him with our inward eye, and determine to stand and fight him hand to hand. If he tells us that we are too weak to fight him, let us tell him that our captain Christ stands with us, and that we fight with the strength of the One who has already defeated him. Let us fence with faith, and comfort ourselves with hope, and smite the devil with the firebrand of charity. Let us take on the mind of our Master, and instead of hating those who kill us, pity them and pray for them in sorrow for the peril they are bringing on themselves. And that firebrand of charity thrown into the devil's face will strike him so suddenly blind that he will not be able to land a stroke on us.

God in his goodness will not fail us. Either he will keep us from suffering, or better still he will give us the strength to endure suffering well. The Lord is being gracious to the one he delivers from all painful trouble; but he is being even more gracious when he allows a man to be delivered from this world through suffering, even by a painful death, and to gain all of heaven's joy. And therefore, let the consideration of all this drive worldly concerns out of your heart, and pray that it may do the same for me.

And with that thought, good cousin, I will end my talking and bid you farewell. For I am beginning to feel a little weary.

VINCENT: A very good place to end indeed, uncle. I am not surprised that you are weary, since I have put you to so much labor. May the Lord reward you for it! I believe that many others will also keep you in their prayers, for I plan to record your words with as much skill as my limited intelligence will allow. And so, praying that God will give to me and the others who read your good counsel the grace to follow it, I will commit you to God.

ANTHONY: I only wish you could have found a wiser man to give you better counsel; and you may still find such a one. But in the meantime I will ask our Lord to breathe his Holy Spirit into the minds and hearts of your readers and inwardly teach them the truth. And so, good cousin, farewell, until God brings us together again, whether here or in heaven.

finis

CLUNY MEDIA

Designed by Fiona Cecile Clarke, the CLUNY MEDIA *logo
depicts a monk at work in the scriptorium,
with a cat sitting at his feet.*

*The monk represents our mission to emulate
the invaluable contributions of the monks
of Cluny in preserving the libraries of the West,
our strivings to know and love the truth.*

*The cat at the monk's feet is Pangur Bán, from the
eponymous Irish poem of the 9th century.
The anonymous poet compares his scholarly
pursuit of truth with the cat's happy hunting of mice.
The depiction of Pangur Bán is an homage to the work
of the monks of Irish monasteries and a sign
of the joy we at Cluny take in our trade.*

"Messe ocus Pangur Bán,
cechtar nathar fria saindan:
bíth a menmasam fri seilgg,
mu memna céin im saincheirdd."